"Sit back with a croissant and an espresso—or better yet, *du vin et du fromage*—and treat yourself to the delights and dilemmas of being a Midwesterner in Paris. Scott Carpenter's tales of life in the French capital will make you laugh, marvel, and daydream about amping up the adventure in your own life. *Merci Monsieur Carpenter!*"

—Lorna Landvik, author of *Chronicles of a Radical Hag*

"Deeply French but also deeply Midwestern—and thus rather perfect."

—Alethea Black, author of *You've Been So Lucky Already*

"*French Like Moi* is not only full of spot-on cultural observations and the laugh-out-loud-yet-self-deprecating humor Minnesotans do so well, it's also beautifully written with a timeless literary flair."

—Heather Stimmler-Hall, author of *Naughty Paris*,
editor of *Secrets of Paris*

"I laughed until my sides hurt at Carpenter's lighthearted and self-deprecating take on living in *l'Hexagone*. For loyal lovers of Paris and France, and anyone who's moved abroad or is thinking about it, *French Like Moi* is a jovial reminder to pack your patience and your dictionary, and gobble up every single, butter-soaked morsel of the journey."

—Kimberley Lovato, author of *Walnut Wine & Truffle Groves*

"Carpenter greets the language, cuisine, culture, and daily details of life with a wit and honesty that makes for a rollicking read. We encounter vivid characters, impossible scenarios, and such hilarious tableaus that soon we all feel French like *lui!*"

—Erin Byrne, author of *Wings: Gifts of Art, Life, and Travel in France*

The most delightful and delicious form of escapism—smart, kind, funny and (best of all!) French. Perfect for Francophiles and dreamers alike.

—K. S. R. Burns, author of *The Paris Effect* and *Paris Ever After*

"A hilarious look at…figuring out life."   —*Readers' Favorite*

Praise for *French Like Moi*

"A delightful read...filled with levity and grace. A winning and witty collection offering humor and insight into the French way of life."

—*Kirkus Reviews*

"*French Like Moi* tours the everyday Paris that's found away from Eiffel Tower tourism. With an entertaining guide at the helm, bon mots and corny puns find a home alongside solid timing, curious anecdotes, and self-aware mocking. This quirky travel memoir uncovers lesser-known facets with verve."

—*Foreword Reviews*, Editor's Pick

"In this funny memoir...Carpenter has a knack for turning potential catastrophes into comedy. Readers will find plenty to appreciate in his sharp take on expat life."

—*Publishers Weekly*

"Carpenter captures the ironies, oddities, and attractions of the French capital in a way few writers have achieved—which is saying a lot, considering how many have tried their hand at conjuring the City of Light.... *French Like Moi* is a delightful romp through French life and Midwestern sensibilities, all combined in one compelling story."

—*Midwest Book Review*

"Loaded with lacerating wit and trenchant but tender observations, Scott Carpenter's *French Like Moi* is also a true original: a serious memoir that doesn't take itself too seriously. It is this humility that gives Carpenter's book its undeniable strength—that, and his vivid, often hilarious storytelling."

—Marcia DeSanctis, New York Times bestselling author of *100 Places in France Every Woman Should Go*

FRENCH LIKE MOI

FRENCH LIKE MOI

A Midwesterner in Paris

SCOTT DOMINIC CARPENTER

TRAVELERS' TALES
AN IMPRINT OF SOLAS HOUSE, INC.

Travelers' Tales and Solas House are trademarks of Solas House, Inc.,
Palo Alto, California
travelerstales.com | solashouse.com

Art Direction: Kimberly Nelson
Cover Design: Kimberly Nelson
Illustrations: Liam Golden
Interior Design and Page Layout: Howie Severson

Library of Congress Cataloging-in-Publication Data is available upon
request.

978-1-60952-183-7 (paperback)
978-1-60952-184-4 (ebook)
978-1-60952-185-1 (hard cover)

First Edition
Printed in the United States
10 9 8 7 6 5 4 3 2 1

For Paul and Muriel.
You guys always have my back.

Table of Contents

A Note on Publication

Acknowledgment is made to the following publications, where various pieces from this book first appeared (often in modified form or under a different title): *The Rumpus*: "French Like Moi" (including the image reproduced in this edition); Mark Twain House Royal Nonesuch Prize: "Squirrel Pie and the Golden Derrière" (later published in *Lowestoft Chronicle*); *Catapult*: "The Medi-Morphosis," "War of the Worlds"; *Ducts*: "Too Soon, Too Close"; *JMWW*: "La Modification"; *Lowestoft Chronicle*: "The Acute and the Grave," "Squirrel Pie and the Golden Derrière"; *Secrets of Paris*: "The Tab," "Underground Man," "Either/Or," "The Cartesian Method."

"What can't you find in a large city
when you know how to walk and how to look?"

—Charles Baudelaire

Rue Babillot

PART ONE

Came

Murders in the
Rue Bobillot

"To be honest," Madame C replied in French, "the problem is the neighbors. They refuse to die."

The comment sent my tea gurgling down the wrong pipe. While I hacked and wheezed, our hostess pinched her brow with concern. Her sandy-haired partner, Patricia, tendered a napkin in case my insides came out.

"*Ça va, Monsieur Carpenter?*"

"*Ça va,*" I croaked, flapping my hand to keep her at bay. Repeating it seemed a good idea. "*Ça va, ça va.*"

Anne, who'd been off inspecting the kitchen, returned to the living room for the chore of pounding her husband on the back. Madame C watched from the sofa, and Patricia added cubes of sugar to their tea. The mood was far from homicidal.

This kind of situation occurred with distressing frequency in Paris: I'd start a conversation on one topic only to find it veering into another. While I squinted at the butcher's explanation about cutlets, the road would somehow fork off to plumbing. At the post office I'd be learning about air mail options, only to feel the clerk had hairpinned to the subject of Etruscan pottery. Swerves like this generally meant I'd misunderstood some crucial word, had careened off the conversational cliff, and had gone airborne for an undetermined amount of time. So, when Madame C mentioned murder as the reason for selling her apartment, I recognized the floating sensation and braced for impact.

Where, I wondered during the fall, had I gone wrong? After all, the verb *mourir* had definitely whizzed by, calling to mind the deathiness of mortgages and mortuaries. And I was pretty sure she'd said something about neighbors. Of course, there'd been a slew of other words, too, some of them possibly significant. It's always hard to tell which parts of a foreign language are the engines and axles, and which are the hood ornaments and air fresheners.

Sometimes, if you play along, you can avoid a crash landing.

"So why do you suppose that is?" I said. "I mean, why is it the neighbors won't…?" And here I made a rolling gesture with my hand, inviting Madame C to fill in the gap with a clarifying comment.

She shrugged. It was inexplicable. Monsieur and Madame Pottard were old and infirm, but they simply "refused."

"You mean they refuse to…?" My hand swirled.

They refused to *partir*, she said—that is, to "leave."

"Like, to an old folks' home?"

"No." Her look went steely. "To the grave."

―――――

Ordinarily that's where this story would end. Madame C's apartment had promise, but I was burdened with these pesky things called principles. I frowned upon stuffing bodies under the floorboards—not just because of the stench, but also on account of it being morally questionable.

Problem was, we were running out of options. After deciding to move our family to Paris, Anne and I had started our search in the center of town. But prices had nudged us outwards, farther and farther into darkness, like NASA's Mariner probe. If Notre-Dame Cathedral represented the center of the Parisian solar system, we were now prospecting between Uranus and Neptune, also known as the thirteenth arrondissement. This was one of the less glamorous parts of the capital, which explained why Madame C's compact abode on the Rue Bobillot was within reach of our budget. It was a tad on the small side—*co-zee* as the realtor put it in his best franglais—but what did we expect? Your average Parisian makes do with quarters the size of an American bedroom. In some parts of town, immigrants carpet their floor with mattresses and sleep in shifts. It doesn't get any more *co-zee* than that.

Which, it turned out, is why they wanted the neighbors dead.

"The apartment is too small for us," Madame C said as Patricia gestured at the walls, nearly spanning them with her outstretched arms. For years now, they'd wanted to buy the place next door and add it on for a little elbow-room. There was just one problem: Monsieur Pottard's stubborn existence.

Madame C raised her arms to the heavens. "The man has had cancer for years. He can barely make it up the stairs."

Patricia chimed in. "And that wife of his!"

"*Mon dieu!* Bedridden as long as we've lived here. A decade! But she won't let go. Neither of them will."

I blinked. It seemed so heartless, so crass, so…well, so much like a French novel.

In *Le Père Goriot*, Balzac proposes a moral test: you can have infinite wealth if you're willing to sacrifice the life of an old fogey in China. Agree to push one geezer off the ledge, and a boundless future is yours. Do you accept? Of course not! But then temptation creeps in. A little infinite wealth could be handy. And China is so far away. Besides, that grandpa might not care. Maybe he's been waiting for someone to give him the old heave-ho.

Madame C had looked this moral quandary in the eye and stared it down. How her fingers must have itched each time that ancient man approached the edge of the stairs.

What to do? We could either enrich this charming murderess or resign ourselves to lesser accommodations—such as a tent below an underpass. Our daughter's socks might get gritty, but at least our conscience would be clear.

The doorbell rang, and Patricia ushered in more shoppers. The wife hadn't even removed her gloves before her eyes went to the woodwork. The husband—a little pucker of a man—was sizing up the walls, framing them in the square of his hands. They were nodding their heads in that *ça va* sort of way. Another thirty seconds and they'd be moving in furniture.

Anne gave me an urgent look, and I concurred.

"We'll take it," we cried.

So began our move to the edge of the fringe of Europe's most glorious capital.

Ah, Paris.

Whether you're talking last tangos, midnights in, red balloons, hunchbacks, French connections, Jean Valjean, *Ratatouille*, or Amélie Poulain, Paris is the place where it all goes down—and where the *it* is big and heart-stopping, something that never leaves you, that you'll always have, like the Paris of *Casablanca*. It's a layered pastry of romance, adventure, and elegance, coated with a glaze of chic!

And also, a tax dodge. Turns out that if you leave the US for most of the year, you glide between the incisors of the IRS. So, when a sabbatical came my way, I dragooned Anne into the idea of France.

Because dragooning was how it had always worked. As a kid my parents had dragooned me into French classes, and when this prepared me for no other career, I was dragooned into teaching the same language to other poor saps, ones who would eventually be dragooned into their own slot in the vicious cycle we call education. To polish my credentials, I'd been dragooning my family for extended stays here for years, lodging us in rat traps, each more squalid than the last.

Buying a place, I contended, meant we'd never again have a dining room table made of plastic. Sitting on the toilet would no longer interfere with shutting the bathroom door. Our kids—well, only our daughter was still at home—could have a dresser instead of a stack of cardboard boxes.

"All that would also be true," Anne pointed out, "if we stayed home."

I love my wife, but her trenchant observations can be a little unbecoming.

"What is it you're really after?" she said. "Why is it so important?"

I struggled for an answer.

"Right," she said. "Let me know when you've figured it out."

All of which led to that day we scribbled our offer on a paper napkin, snatching up Madame C's apartment before the other couple could unholster their wallet.

On our way out we crossed paths with a twig-like man heaving a pull-cart of groceries up the stairs. It was none other than Monsieur Pottard, the old man whose life we were in the process of saving. Since we'd soon be living next door, I introduced myself and offered him a hand with his burden.

When the poor fellow clutched his heart in surprise, I realized my mistake: I'd taken this man for a *neighbor* when he was, instead, a *voisin*.

In the Midwest, neighbors tend to be chatty folks who wave from their barbecue. They'll lend you a cup of sugar or rent out their kid to mow your lawn. But a French *voisin* is a different creature altogether. He may live next door, but that's his fault, not yours. Proximity is the mother of contempt. A good *voisin* should leave you the hell alone, and the

best *voisin* is a dead one—especially if his passing allows you to purchase his apartment and blow out a wall.

Which explained why my offer of assistance pushed Monsieur Pottard to the brink of cardiac arrest.

I leaned forward. "*Ça va, Monsieur Pottard?*"

"*Oui,*" he croaked, "*ça va.*"

Ça va. "It goes." This expression is the Swiss Army knife of the French language. When used as a question (*ça va?*), the phrase contains its own answer (*ça va!*). Moreover, it can bat away any query slung in your direction. Should a pal inquire how your weekend was, you can shrug and say *ça va*, which means, "It was OK, but nothing special." If the rental car guy asks if you'd like a green Renault, *ça va* will again do the trick, communicating that the vehicle will be satisfactory. Should someone offer you a second serving of calf brains at dinner, you can pause, reflect, and say, *ça va, merci,* which translates as "I couldn't eat another bite, thank you." And if ever the questions get too hard (Who's the president of France? How do you like your eggs?), there's a special peremptory version that goes *Oh! ça va!* You hold up both palms at the same time, and this means "Enough with the questions already."

The phrase has no English equivalent, which is a common manufacturing defect in French. Even simple things here have a way of turning strange. For example, *un car* is pretty obviously a car—until it turns out to be a bus. *Un coin* is not a coin, but a corner, and the word *actuellement* doesn't actually mean "actually." (It means "at present.")

French is filled with elephant traps such as these—deep pits masked by foliage, with stakes pointing up from the bottom, ready to shish-kebab foreigners as they topple in. Some of the pits get rather crowded.

How is it down here? the newly impaled ones ask.

Oh, someone drawls from the darkness, *ça va.*

And it's not just language. Lots of things in France are weird, and it's up to you to determine which ones are genuinely strange and which are just the way they do it here.

For example, to buy Madame C's apartment, we needed a mortgage. Back in the States, mortgage bankers resemble parole officers, severe and world-weary. So, when our Parisian banker looked like a debonair middle schooler—the cuffs of his navy-blue suit coming down to his hairless knuckles—it made me wonder: cultural difference, or just your run-of-the-mill bad idea?

When I asked this youngster if he had any experience with foreigners buying property, he swept away my concerns like so many crumbs.

"*Ça va aller, Monsieur Carpenter!*" he scoffed, deploying a variation on the standard expression—not "it's going" in the present, but "it's *going* to go," sometime, maybe, in the future. All would be fine, he assured me, as long as I filled out the forms without error, provided copies of documents that do not exist in the US, and coughed up the appropriate fees.

Meanwhile, another person was demanding documents: the *notaire*.

Now, to the American brain, this one seems obvious enough: if an *adversaire* is an adversary, and a *salaire* is a salary, then surely a *notaire* must be a notary.

Welcome to the elephant pit! You've just landed on a special skewer—where the translation is both right and wrong at the same time.

In the States a notary is a person who bought himself a rubber stamp on the internet, whereas the French *notaire* is a creature with supernatural powers—a kind of Frankenstein's monster, stitched together from lawyers and bureaucrats, joined at the wallet. They specialize in real estate and wills, and it's impossible to purchase property or die without their assistance.

Our *notaire* was Maître Le Bivic, and the man cut a suave figure in his office on the rare occasions he was present. The walls were decorated with pictures of the Breton coast, replete with lighthouses and sailboats, including one particularly elegant two-master that hinted at what our fees were paying for. Clerks swarmed about like deck hands.

I should clarify that Maître was not his first name. You address a notary as Master, which leaves you feeling a bit like Gollum.

While straightening his cufflinks, Master Le Bivic explained the steps—the required documents and the waiting periods, and how the two *notaires* representing buyer and seller would engage in shuttle diplomacy, as though annexing a small nation.

Americans like things to be snappy, and in the US it's possible to close a real-estate transaction in a couple of days. In France, however, the process takes at least six months. After all, Paris was settled long before Julius Caesar added it to the map of the Roman Empire, so the title search alone can take a while. Then there are tests to be performed—geometers measuring the surface area down to the closest centimeter, pest controllers checking for termites and rats, technicians detecting lead levels. Is the ground under the building riddled with old quarries? Are fungi blooming in the walls? How's the asbestos doing?

The master squinted as he read the legal description of our apartment. "Are you sure it's big enough for you?" he asked. His eyes wandered to the yacht pictured above our heads, the cabin of which was undoubtedly larger.

Well, yes, our new home might be a little *co-zee*, I conceded. "*Mais ça va.*"

Over the coming months I collected documents and made pilgrimages to the bank, always providing an American approximation of what had been requested: salary stubs, tax returns, bank statements. Ensconced in his basement office, the child banker leafed through the papers and promised to send them up the line for review.

"How long will that take?" I asked.

"*Ne vous inquiétez pas, Monsieur Carpenter.*"

I tried not to disquiet myself, and he emitted his condescending chuckle. "It's going," he assured us. "It's going to go."

While the cogs of banking turned, we revisited the apartment to measure for furniture. The place seemed to have shrunk since our first visit. Where exactly was our daughter going to sleep? Anne and I ran into each other at the doorway, replaying a scene from Laurel and Hardy. The hacking cough of bedridden Madame Pottard rattled through the walls.

As we left, we found her husband roaming the landing, a bit lost, his eyes huge behind the inch-thick glasses. I took it upon myself to point him in the right direction. After all, once you've saved a person's life, they become your responsibility.

Anne gave me a look. Was moving here really worth it?

It was a fair question. Fact is, France is often a pain. And I so clearly don't belong. As a tall-ish person with Germanic features and sloppy American posture, my nationality has never been much of a secret in these parts. Usually I attract attention I don't want—and not just from pickpockets and beggars.

Even after all my years in the country, people still introduced me at dinner parties as so-and-so's *American friend*, the way you might whisper to guests that the creature joining the meal is actually a Martian or a Lutheran, just to forewarn everyone about the odd behaviors. Sometimes I'd catch people trying to talk over my head, the way grownups ixnay their way through risqué topics when a child is in the room. Conversely, whenever conversation turned to transatlantic events, heads rotated in my direction: I was always expected to have an opinion.

What I wanted most of all was to fit in, and the key to this was to act as if nothing surprised me. So, I affected Parisian nonchalance. When Madame C confessed she wished to kill her neighbors, I nodded with sympathy. When she lied about the square footage of the apartment we were buying, I shrugged. And when our adolescent banker told me week after week that everything was fine, I concealed the fact that the bladder of my worries was overfull.

Following this principle of insouciance, I nodded like a bobble-head doll as Master Le Bivic walked us through the draft of the contract of sale.

Ça va? he asked occasionally, and I responded in kind. After all, *ça va* is the expression of non-surprise par excellence, ranking with the English greats, such as *sure, whatever,* and—where I hail from—*you betcha.*

The strategy seemed to work. Whenever something weird went down, I'd check the folks around me for a hint of raised eyebrow. If they didn't flinch, then why should I? Bit by bit I gave myself over to the wisdom of the group, like a lemming who sees his pals out for a jog and hustles out to join them.

On the day before the closing, I returned to the bank. My baby-faced loan officer sat at his desk, pale in the fluorescent light, and for the first time, two other people stood in the room—middle-aged managerial types with sour-faces.

"*Bonjour*," I sang out, a tremolo in my voice. How, I asked, was it going?

The boy in the suit raised his palms in defense. "*Ah, Monsieur Carpenter. Ça ne va pas.*"

It stunned me to hear the expression in the negative. He repeated it, adding a kicker.

"*Non, ça ne va pas du tout.*"

One of the managers wrenched open the boy's desk drawer, and my documents spilled to the floor. Turned out things weren't *going*, and weren't ever *going to go*, precisely because my file had never *gone* anywhere.

All at once, while the imp in the too-large coat sat twiddling his thumbs, I understood my miscalculation. Through all the realtors, sellers, inspectors, and *notaires*, I'd been watching for cultural difference, translating the neighboring shades of meaning—only to forget the one irreducible kernel that transcends all cultures and all times, that manifests itself in every place and every language, that blunts the edge of all weapons, the only true universal: incompetence.

A bleak future loomed. We were missing the date, the sale would fall through, our earnest money would evaporate.

They say men are too proud to admit their errors, but really it's a logistical problem: where would we find time to confess to them all? When I told Anne how I'd squandered our meager fortune, she gave me a frank look, folding her arms across her chest.

"Stop moping," she ordered, "and do something about it." She has always had the tedious job of playing the grownup in our marriage.

So I *did* do something: I groveled before the master and begged *him* to do something. Luckily, *notaires* enjoy opportunities to flex their omnipotence. He flew into action, made a few calls, unfurled the silkiness of his voice. A date was changed, a favor called in. And suddenly things were back on track.

"*Voilà*," Master Le Bivic said, rolling his hand open as though a dove might appear on his palm.

Days later we arrived at our new home on the Rue Bobillot and unlocked the door into emptiness, our voices echoing off the barren walls. The place had been skinned alive— Madame C having taken not only the light fixtures, but also the appliances, the curtains, even the kitchen cabinets. I checked to make sure the copper pipes were still in the walls.

The plaster was pocked and the floors dirty, but at least it was *our* plaster, *our* filth, *our* home. *Chez nous.*

Two of our friends helped us move in. They paused at the door until Guy cleared his throat and declared it *très bien.*

"Right," Sabine quipped. "If you're a midget."

The space filled quickly. The bedroom door knocked against the dresser, the sofa fit only at an angle. Each time we emptied a box, I flattened it to make room for our feet. For a few hours we scrubbed, crumpled, jammed, and scooted—puzzling each piece into place. At the end, Anne found the corkscrew, and we opened a bottle to celebrate our exhaustion.

A hacking cough sounded through the wall, followed by a wheeze. The neighbors' TV blared. We heard their bed squeak.

The next day I bumped into Monsieur Pottard on the landing. The husk of a man stood tethered to his pull-cart, uncertain before the series of doors. His hollow stare somehow reminded me of Balzac, of temptation, of that anonymous old geezer in China.

I returned to the cramped shell we now called home, banging my elbows in the entryway. It was so exceedingly *co-zee.* What had we been thinking? The future narrowed.

Another cough rattled through the paper-thin plaster, and I stared at the wall for a long time. How easily it could come down—if ever the opportunity presented itself.

A serpent hissed in my ear. How long would it be?

After all, those neighbors, they couldn't last forever. The stairs were steep. The floors were freshly waxed. And no matter how careful you are, accidents happen.

A shiver ran through me, and I couldn't un-think the thought. What had I become?

Then I realized: I was fitting in.

And how did I feel about that?

Well, I thought, *ça va.*

Either/Or

OUR NEW NEIGHBORHOOD WAS CLOTTED with eateries, including one of those intimate, white-linen affairs—the kind that makes you dig your necktie out of the mothballs, where even the busboys out-dress you, and your finest shoes feel like clodhoppers. Our friend Guy had recommended this particular establishment, his voice aquiver and his eyes narrowing to slits as he reminisced about the food.

Anne made a reservation, and as we counted down the days, the cornucopia of possibilities swelled. Roman banquet tables came to mind, the kind where you gorge yourself on suckling boar, towers of pastry, and platters of wine-smothered songbirds. Maybe there'd be an orgy, too. I've heard they're good for digestion.

It was thus with some consternation that we opened the leather-bound menus that night and found nothing between the covers.

It bears explaining that in Paris most restaurants offer two ways to go. You can select dishes helter-skelter without restriction (known as ordering *à la carte*), or else go for the fixed menu, the package deal. Here, however, we had neither. Framed in calfskin was a card the size of a wedding invitation. The calligraphed text welcomed us to our dining experience, and it named the chef. And at the bottom there showed a number almost long enough to be a date, but which, upon examination, appeared to be a price.

I hailed a passing waiter, a thin fellow with slicked-back hair and a napkin draped over his sleeve. "Excuse me," I said. "But there's no menu in the menu."

The man pressed his fingertips together with indulgence, explaining how that was the point. Dishes were not listed because, in fact, they had not yet been invented. We were invited to give ourselves over to the fantasies of the resident culinary magician, who would produce a succession of micro-courses for our delight.

"But what will they be?" I said.

He gave me a prim look. "A surprise."

At first I balked. Rolling the dice at mealtime puts me on edge. When dinner is at stake, I want to win every time.

And yet, a weight rose from my shoulders. I felt... relieved. The fact is, there's nothing harder to read in France than a restaurant menu. In the fancier joints you'd be better off picking through hieroglyphs than trying to decipher the regional names for bird parts or pig organs. Wine lists are even worse: pages and pages that read like *War and Peace* in the original Russian.

At this establishment, however, they had reduced choice to its very atom: you dined here or you didn't. Beyond that, your input was superfluous, like eating at my mom's.

Americans have a hard time giving up their choices. I'd noticed this before, when taking visitors out to the brasserie close to our apartment. "What kind of fries do they have?" my brother-in-law once asked as he scowled through the menu. He expected a choice between curly fries, steak fries, waffle fries, crinkle fries, and, I don't know, maybe even onion rings. "Just fries," I told him. "You know, the regular ones." When we got to salad dressing, I didn't have the heart to confess there was only one. Instead, I agreed to order him the French version of Thousand Island. Luckily, he was on his third beer by the time the evidence appeared before him.

I used to be like that, too, but spending so much time in France has made me soft. The little organ in charge of choosing has atrophied. Now when I'm in the States, I tire of playing twenty questions every time I have a meal, and my personal vision of hell resembles a Subway restaurant where a teenager with sniffles stands behind an infinitely long counter. The demon starts his torture with an initial question: "What kind of bread?"

Americans are partial to choice because that's how we're brought up. We learn the *à la carte* mentality in school, where kids get to make up their own projects and select from a smorgasbord of sports. In some books they can even choose their own adventure, skipping about the pages and deciding how they'd like the story to unfold. They get to have their way with everything.

And after high school it gets even worse. Whenever I explain American colleges to friends in Paris, their mouths form little O's, and it takes them a moment to construct a question that isn't too insulting. *Where's the rigor?* they sputter. *Why does American education sound so much like a cafeteria—one filled with junk food?* And most of all, *Why would you let students make so many choices before they're even educated?* I tell them about my own experience as an undergraduate, where I changed majors every semester, even during senior year. Once, just to test the limits, I declared Mortuary Science on my registration card. But French people don't chuckle at this anecdote. They shake their heads, in much the same way my dad did.

Probably that's because French schools shut down options as fast as they can. Their philosophy is to get rid of the clutter. Don't bother with what's irrelevant. At eleven or twelve a French kid's future starts closing in on him. Students here are like rats in a special maze—one where every time you turn a corner, a wall appears behind you to keep you from backing up. Like Napoleon's troops, French rats keep marching forward.

By contrast, American rats charge at random, ramming into walls, scratching at corners. When one path is blocked, they double back and try another, and then another—whatever it takes to get the cheese.

And it's not just education. A lot of France is offered as a fixed menu. That's what immigrants discover all the time: you can take or leave it, but there won't be any substitutions. It's great if you happen to have a hankering for what they're serving. But who knows? Maybe you were brought up on a different diet. Maybe nuts make your throat swell, or gluten twists your gut. Then you might find the local stuff hard to swallow.

It's not always pleasurable to be relieved of options. When I was a kid, the dinner table rule was *you'd better get used to it because that's what we're having.* In France, though, the elimination of choice comes from a place of confidence. *Don't bother asking*, the chef seems to say, *because what's coming will be better than anything you can imagine.*

So it was that night at the restaurant. A succession of dainty plates came before us, with a supporting cast of gold and ruby wines. Our first steps into the meal were tentative and awkward, the way you start a blind date. We prodded at bubbles of gelatin and picked suspiciously at pastry. Over time, our confidence grew. Soon we were guessing at ingredients. Shapes and colors fed our eyes. We marveled at the phrasing. And then, every time they cleared a plate and presented a new bewilderment, I felt a flutter. It was a shiver of suspense—that lush pleasure of giving in or giving over, of allowing yourself to be seduced by someone who understands your appetites better than you do yourself.

Which system, I wondered, is preferable—total choice or none at all? French people get cattle-prodded down a single chute, and not all of them like it. On the other hand,

Americans with too much leeway end up wandering like stray cats.

It went on for ten courses that night, each more sensuous than the last. A square of sea bass evaporated on my tongue. The medallion of lamb made my lip quiver. I'd come hoping for an unbridled orgy of taste, only to find the roles reversed, as if dinner were devouring me.

Dessert was pornographic: a cube of mango sorbet draped with chestnut sauce, the entire affair captured within a transparent dome of sugar. I tapped the confection with my spoon, and a glitter of sweetness showered down.

That's when I knew what I craved: a chef dressed like a dominatrix, one who would strip away choice, thrash me with goodies, subjugate me. I wanted the cracking whip of surprise, the shiver of risk. I longed for the absence of control.

But still, me being me, I also wanted a safeword.

La Modification

Paris changes, poet Charles Baudelaire wrote, faster than the human heart, and as far as our neighborhood is concerned, he was right. We'd barely moved into the thirteenth arrondissement before people were tearing things up.

Usually it started in the morning. A flatbed truck would wheel around the corner, and three men in coveralls would hop off. From our living room, I'd watch them take a pickaxe to the asphalt. A team like this could dig an eight-foot trench in two days, after which they'd replace a nut on a water main and fill the hole back up. Sometimes they'd tinker with phone lines or unearth electrical cables. Often their labors led to nothing at all: I'd see crews slice through the skin of the street and rummage lengthily in the guts before sealing it all up again, a look of vague confusion on their faces, like doctors who'd failed to locate a major organ. No sooner did they finish tamping gravel into the freshly poured tar than the gas people would arrive and rip it all open again, eager to satisfy the neighborhood's craving for spools of yellow tubing.

27

There were other projects, too. Scaffolding went up and down, rubble accumulated outside doorways, men crawled about rooftops. Up the street a building had started to split in two, prompting a crew to strap a kind of girdle to the thing.

Then fate took a more ominous turn. In front of our building there lies a wedge-shaped square containing four chestnut trees, and one morning a truck backed its way over the curb onto the raised center. Men in blue coveralls unloaded sheets of corrugated metal and built a work enclosure the size of our apartment, as tightly wrapped as a Christo installation. From the truck came tools—shovels, jackhammers, wheelbarrows— all of which disappeared with the men behind the barrier.

Noises ensued.

In the weeks since we'd moved in, no one had excavated our little square, and now it felt like an intrusion. What on earth were they up to?

I, too, had been digging, albeit in a less literal way. The goal was to learn about our new environment—its habits and mechanisms. Of course, that was only during my free time. Now that teaching was over, I mostly reported to my "summer boss," who was back in the States with our daughter to tie up loose ends. Anne managed me from afar, sending detailed instructions for getting the apartment in shape before their return, when the three of us would start our first year living in the sardine can we called home.

I spent a lot of time scratching my head, contemplating collapsible furniture for the tight quarters. Maybe there were beds you could winch to the ceiling. Whenever I ran out of ideas, I took a break and spied on the neighborhood.

During the workweek you could set your clock by small events. It all started around 7:30 A.M., when the homeless guy down the street crawled from his sleeping bag. He'd wander over to a wall and stand as if chatting with the bricks while water pooled by his feet. It was important that he keep to his schedule, because soon schoolkids would come pattering by, briefcase-like bags strapped to their shoulders. Next it was the bigger ones, ten or twelve years old, traveling in pairs or threesomes, sometimes with cigarettes dangling from their prepubescent lips. Down at the corner the crossing guard in her chartreuse vest performed semaphore with puppet-sized stop signs. In the street, the ballet of cars got underway. The mailwoman rolled her cart along the sidewalk, and lights flickered on at the handbag shop.

However, the new project on our square wasn't part of the usual schedule, and the metal enclosure gave it an air of mystery. Because leaves from the chestnut trees obscured my view, I headed downstairs for a fuller inspection.

In the stairwell I encountered the cadaverous Monsieur Pottard. Now, back in the Midwest, I tend to smile at others when they cross my path, and I use more greetings than are strictly necessary. However, this kind of free-wheeling friendliness is not the tradition in Paris, so my *bonjour* triggered a gasp of surprise from our octogenarian neighbor, leaving him teetering on the landing. Bumping *into* the poor

fellow felt alarmingly close to bumping him *off*, which was enough to make me daydream about that easily removable wall separating our apartments. Today, though, I spared him and continued on my path.

To plumb the mystery of the new worksite, I knocked at the door of the neighbors I knew best—our concierge and his wife, Monsieur and Madame Carvalho. Because they'd lived in the building for thirty years, the Carvalhos always had the low-down, especially on such matters as who emptied their trash after hours, who tracked mud up the stairs, and who jammed the buttons on the elevator—although certain details were often lost to me in the folds of their Portuguese accents, especially when Madame Carvalho grew excited.

As luck would have it, the husband answered the door.

"Do you know what they're doing out on the square?" I asked.

"*Sais pas*," Monsieur Carvalho replied with a shrug. It was the first time I'd heard him stumped by a question of this sort. Together we stepped out to the curb, the better to watch and speculate. The enclosure of corrugated metal was a good eight feet tall, so there wasn't much to examine. But the groan of machinery confirmed that change was underway.

Usually, vehicles associated with street projects bore the logo of the gas or phone company, but this time the signage pointed to a different culprit: the city itself, which is to say the mayor of our arrondissement, who is to the mayor of Paris as a cardinal is to the pope. The involvement of local government suggested that something big had befallen us—more than a mere repair. Perhaps we were about to receive a coveted plot of grass. Or even, it occurred to me, a Wallace Fountain, one of those cast iron affairs where small Roman figurines stand on a pedestal, holding a dome over burbling water. My imagination tingled. It might even be—but surely this was too much to hope for—a *newsstand*, which, aside from enhancing the picturesqueness on view from my living room window, would save me an extra thirty paces whenever I felt the urge to know what was going on in the world.

Some such cultural improvement would be welcome. After all, our neighborhood wasn't exactly the tourist hub of Paris. In a pinch, you could make postcards of it, but you'd have to be pretty good with Photoshop. Many parts of the capital were designed with great vistas in mind, but the thirteenth arrondissement wasn't one of them. Back in the nineteenth century, when the Second Empire decided to fix the medieval mess that passed for Paris, they razed whole blocks of buildings to make broad boulevards, often plopping things like opera houses at the end to give you something to look at. But in the southeast section of town, we came through that period of improvements pretty much unscathed. I didn't expect any miracles, but it seemed the city had finally gotten around to us, preparing some minor embellishment I might admire from my living room window.

Otherwise, most of the neighborhood sights were eyesores, a kind of caricature of the Paris that people imagine. Downtown they had Notre-Dame Cathedral, whereas all we had was Sainte-Anne church, a cement behemoth whose collapsing ribs conveyed the sense that the heavens were falling. Instead of the Louvre, our neighborhood sported an impressive collection of graffiti. The luxury hotels of the center were replaced here by low-income housing. And in lieu of the Champs-Elysées...well, there we didn't really have anything.

The same was true of the residents. If you're walking in the trendy parts—say, the Boulevard Saint-Germain—you quickly get the impression that Parisian women have second careers as magazine models, and that most men spend their days grooming. Our neighborhood, on the other hand, sported an alarming clutter of real people. In our building, for instance, I frequently encountered Monsieur Monot, a massive creature the shape and color of the Incredible Hulk—if you imagine the superhero having weathered middle age on a diet of Budweiser and Fritos. Too large for the tiny elevator, Monsieur Monot wheezed up several flights of stairs each day, groceries in hand, rivulets of sweat drenching his tent-like shirt. He wasn't the only non-traditional figure. Most days, around mid-morning, a man with Einstein hair wandered down the sidewalk across the street, quarreling with himself while batting at the air. Next came the physical anomalies. A pair of dwarfs passed by on market days, and you'd encounter a surprising number of folks in wheelchairs. In our neighborhood so many people walked with canes or crutches that I wondered if we'd moved in next to an institute for the feeble-limbed.

Sometimes I was offered other slices of life. One day I saw a mother arguing with her young son, who was hopping with impatience. Then she faced him to the wall of a building and pulled down his shorts. Soon a stream of water ran between his shoes. Seeing this was rather like learning a new word: suddenly instances of it were everywhere. Little boys were constantly in the process of relieving themselves. More than once I saw a father suspend a little girl over the gutter so that she could do her version of the same thing.

In the Midwest we're trained to hold it in till our eyeballs go yellow. But in Paris, apparently anything goes. I thought of the morning ritual of the homeless man up the street. This is how it begins. Your mother makes you pee against a wall, and your future is sealed.

There were other assaults on picturesqueness. For example, our street had an abundance of vagrants, known locally as *clochards*. One morning I went out to find an unshaven specimen sitting on a piece of cardboard outside the door of our bakery, his deeply lined face framed by curly hair. He wore a winter coat, but in honor of the July heat, he'd left it unzipped over his T-shirt. A plastic bowl sat before his outstretched legs, seeded with a few coins. Next to it stood a small sign reading: *j'ai fin*—a gravely poetic wording that suggested he had reached the limit of what a man could bear: *I have end*. Then I recognized it as the misspelling of a more common but equally poignant phrase: *j'ai faim*, "I am hungry."

"*Bonjour*," he said pleasantly.

"*Bonjour*," I replied. It seemed the thing to say. After all, he was chummier than most of my building-mates, and after a few weeks of living solo, I was lonely.

He chinned toward the square, where construction continued behind the curtain of corrugated metal. "What are they building?"

"I don't know."

He nodded. Another of life's mysteries.

The conversation had stalled, so I stepped over his legs to get to the door. There were croissants to be purchased.

Inside, I greeted our bakery ladies and placed my order. I half-expected them to mention the man outside, the one trying to skim small change from their customers. After all, the ladies and I often shared small confidences—about the weather, for instance, or creampuffs. But neither of them brought up this new topic. Was it possible they hadn't noticed? While the blond one twisted my pastries in a sheet of paper, I pondered my duty. Surely they would want to know about any interference with their business. Besides, a good deed of this sort would strengthen our bond.

I leaned over the counter. "Just so you know," I murmured, "there is a man seated outside your door." I leaned farther. "He is asking for money."

I'm not sure what reaction I expected from this announcement. Not thanks, exactly, but perhaps some expression of shared exasperation. *Good grief*, they might say. *Not again*. After all, it could hardly be good for business to have such a shabby creature mooching at your door. People would go and buy their croissants at the bakery down the street.

"Well," said the brunette with a shrug. "He has to sit somewhere, doesn't he?"

Suddenly I felt very small.

The French tolerance for the scruffy and unhinged of the world hadn't entirely eluded me. Paris is unforgiving of small social infractions, but once you cross a certain threshold, almost any eccentricity can be pardoned—sort of the way that, in the US, petty thieves get thrown in prison while the more ambitious ones are put in charge of hedge funds. Down the street a group of fragrant men congregated every day on a bench to drink beer until afternoon nap time. An especially optimistic member of this crew—a fellow with pasta-encrusted whiskers and only one leg—set himself up next to an ATM, where he waited for handouts from people making withdrawals. You had to admire the chutzpah of it. I never saw anyone offer him one of their crisp twenties or fifties, but that didn't seem to bother him. It was like the lottery: you don't win often, but when you do, you win big.

The construction project on the square provided entertainment for these *clochards*, and three or four of them watched daily from a bench while workmen pushed wheelbarrows and carried tubes. The mere spectacle of this activity seemed to heighten their thirst, and often I'd find one or two of these men in line before me at the supermarket, counting out panhandled centimes for their next can or two of happiness.

So much beer was going in that I started wondering where it was all coming out. An alleyway next to the church saw a lot of action, and sometimes there'd be strange puddles on the sidewalk, even on bone-dry days. Somehow this was less cute than when the toddlers did it.

Still, it wasn't entirely their fault: peeing is a problem in this city. People love all the small shops in Paris until they realize how hard that makes it to slip in to use the facilities. A friend of mine travels with a list of the larger hotels, ones where your trespassing into their lobby won't arouse suspicion. You can always stop at a café, of course, but then you need to order some kind of beverage, which gives another push to the vicious cycle of urination.

In our neighborhood the derelicts deal with such problems matter-of-factly, and I admire their authenticity. Our vagrants are the real deal—so much better than what you find in the center of town, where, frankly, you never quite know what you're getting in the *clochard* department. In tourist areas, you happen upon hordes of begging women, often with infants— or at least infant-like bundles—in their arms. Men in that part of town tend to beg in the company of dogs. Either way, the animals and children are intended to tenderize the hearts of passersby—and sometimes to distract you while a colleague lifts your wallet. On the more heavily traveled sections of the Metro you are often treated (once the doors have closed) to a declaration of poverty by a man or woman who needs your assistance. The problem is, you never know for sure who is the genuine article, and rumors circulate about skillful beggars who pull down big money and keep a room at the George V.

Where I live, though, the down-and-out come with the neighborhood. They commandeer the benches along the street and invite you to part with spare change. One fellow opens the door of the church for people willing to test their faith against the falling chunks of ceiling. Whenever his palm has filled with coins, he staggers off to the supermarket for another can of redemption.

Back on our square, behind the corrugated metal, work progressed in fits and starts. It was late July now, hot, and the city moved more slowly. Occasionally I'd find old Monsieur Pottard standing dazed in the hallway, and I'd resist the temptation to check him for a pulse. The vast Monsieur Monot grunted his way up the stairs, sweat streaming down his necks.

Outside, days passed when no workers showed up at all. Then there'd be a spurt of activity, and a crew of municipal Oompa-Loompas in blue coveralls would trudge back and forth.

One day I came home to find Monsieur Carvalho waiting for me. He was excited. A truck had come by, he said, delivering a gigantic crate to the construction site. I peeked through the cracks in the fencing, and it was true: a kiosk-like shape sat in the middle of the space, eight feet tall, and wrapped in a tarpaulin.

The idea of the newsstand was rekindled. But this new structure seemed almost too large. Might it be some kind of concession? What about a theater for marionettes? Surely it wouldn't be anything so grand as a monument. Probably. One thing was sure: our little square would never be the same. The neighborhood was being offered a hub, an attraction, a gift.

The point had not been lost on the *clochards*. A large audience of them showed up each day to watch. My curly-haired friend—the one posted outside the bakery—seemed intrigued too, in a meditative way.

I'd gotten used to this fellow. I'd begun thinking of him as "my" *clochard*, as if he'd been put up for adoption. And it occurred to me that he could help with a problem I had—namely, pennies. The damn things were accumulating rapidly in the change bowl on my dresser upstairs—possibly even breeding. So one day I bent down and deposited a handful of them into his bowl, rather pleased to have discovered an act of charity that rid me of something I didn't want in the first place. It was altruism without the price. My plan was to clear out my stock of centimes little by little, purchasing a daily rush of self-satisfaction on the cheap.

"Hey," the guy said, looking at my alms. "What do you think you're doing? This isn't a dumping ground."

And thus I was shamed into offering larger coins, and more frequently.

Occasionally my snooping was interrupted by calls from the boss. Anne wanted progress reports. Our daughter would have preferred regress reports—that is, some sign that we'd come to our senses and weren't really going to conscript her into a French eighth grade. I confirmed that things were "ship shape." Which was pretty much true if your ship was in dry dock, only half-constructed.

In addition to having my very own *clochard*, I also now had "my" butcher shop, "my" produce vendor, "my" barber, "my" café, "my" wine merchant. In the sweltering July heat I toted my groceries up the stairs, and when I passed the neighbors, they sometimes mumbled a greeting. Even Monsieur Monot, that great human gourd, gave the occasional nod as he huffed up the stairs.

Repetition forged relationships. The newspaper vendor knew what to ring up before I made it through the door. The bakery lady and I played a little game each day where she'd ask what I wanted as she reached for the object of my desire. The barber checked to make sure I wanted *the same cut as last time*. Even old Monsieur Pottard, his unblinking eyes magnified by the glasses, sometimes uttered a greeting in the hallway.

I'd finally broken through the social crust. *The* neighborhood was turning into *my* neighborhood. You could hear it in the way people greeted me. No dictionary can capture the endless permutations to which the word *bonjour* is subject. Now clipped and cold, now playful and filled with song, these two syllables can tell whole novels, the vowels alone containing a thousand shades of meaning. I was getting the whole symphony. Yes, Paris changes. The proof was that the neighborhood had absorbed me.

I celebrated this victory one day with a long stroll across my territory, all the way through Chinatown, coming out close to the ring road, where I stopped in a café for a beer. It was twilight when I headed home—one of those cloudless evenings when the breeze is hot but dry. The sky had gone purple, a few of the bolder stars already glinting. The universe stretched overhead, heavenly bodies bound by invisible strands—like the woof and weave that envelope us all. It was one of those moments when you feel you are part of a vast communion of souls.

I passed a young woman on the street, and out of nowhere she uttered *bonsoir*—not the impersonal, shopkeeper version, but something more fragrant and familiar. *We're all in this together*, her tone said. *We are human beings on a common adventure.* I walked now with a lighter step. Sometimes the heavens aligned. Things could fit. Two people crossing paths on a sidewalk in a huge city could sense their shared humanity—the fleeting pleasure of intersecting lives.

"Bonsoir," another woman called from the darkness.

It was catching! I glanced back and we exchanged a smile. "*Bonsoir!*" I sang, infusing the word with emotion. *You are fresh and beautiful*, my greeting communicated. *In another life, who knows what might have been?* The moment was ripe with possibility, and its passing would remain with both of us forever.

"Bonsoir," a third voice rang out as I danced ahead. This girl was heavier. She wore a leather skirt, and her fishnet stockings led to stiletto heels.

Then I understood and my shoulders rounded. As night fell, the prostitutes had slunk out like cats.

Something stirred below my belt, and I shrank with horror. What kind of monster was I? But no, it was less the sensation of pleasure than of pressure. The beer I'd drunk was completing its passage south. I needed to get home, or soon I'd be joining the ranks of the *clochards*.

August was a difficult, stifling month. Construction out on the square ground to a halt. Shops closed for vacation. Friends and neighbors fled town for the countryside or beach. New furniture sat in our apartment for days, still in its plastic. I called home while sitting on the floor, Chinese food cartons stacked by my knee. In my dreams I joined my family in Minnesota, but each morning I woke in Paris, twisted in sweat-soaked sheets, the air humming with heat. Even the curly-haired vagrant from the bakery had disappeared. Probably he'd earned a couple weeks on the Riviera.

Then, one day, I saw Monsieur Carvalho muttering with a policeman downstairs. The officer scribbled notes on a pad, and the word *mort* drifted in my direction. Dead! A horror rose in me, followed by a sudden shameful thrill. It had to be Monsieur Pottard! To think I'd seen the old man just a day ago, and now...and now...the fleetingness of existence weighed upon me. But at the same time two grubbing words hissed in my ear: *the apartment! the apartment!*

"*Qu'est-ce qui se passe?*" a creaking voice asked, and I jumped to find Monsieur Pottard standing next to me, looking less dead than expected, a head of lettuce in the crook of his arm.

No, it was Monsieur Monot, the Hulk, who had expired from the heat. Getting the body down the stairs had been quite an operation.

Yes, Paris changed. The city was a moving target. I couldn't keep up.

Finally August ended. The cycle started anew, similar but different. School-aged kids reappeared, tanned and older now. The mailwoman had been replaced by a mailman. The crossing guard in the chartreuse vest had put on weight.

In a week my family would return. As if to prepare for their imminent arrival, the workmen suddenly re-appeared on the square, scurrying to complete the neighborhood surprise. Soon the smell of new asphalt seeped through the corrugated enclosure. The flatbed truck came back, and the men in coveralls loaded their tools. Finally the panels of metal disappeared, dismantled sheet by sheet—like the laborious unwrapping of a Christmas present.

The oblong structure stood eight feet tall in the middle of the square, as smooth as a space capsule, as inscrutable as a time machine—a windowless chamber of privacy people could visit one at a time.

It would prove to be a great attraction. From my living room window, through the leaves of the chestnut trees, I'd catch glimpses of arriving visitors. One by one they'd come to our modest installation, sighing like pilgrims at the end of their journey. The chamber was a great leveler, appeal-ing to women laden with shopping bags, men in business suits, schoolchildren, teenagers, old folks with canes, lost tourists growing desperate—and yes, even our beggars, our little menagerie of *clochards*, who would rise from the bench from time to time to visit it again, never tiring of this great offering of the city.

Our new public toilet was open for business.

City of Light Bulbs

SURPRISE IS THE HIGHEST FORM OF PLEASURE, and it's easier to find than people think. You don't have to invest your 401(k) in Powerball numbers to enjoy the fruits of unpredictability, or even travel by Amtrak. No, it turns out you can simply move to Paris, where the ordinary so often leads to adventure.

It went like this. Shortly before Anne returned from the States, I finished painting the walls and pushing the furniture back in place. During my final check, I discovered the bedroom lamp had burnt out. This led me to hoof it to the local supermarket, which stocks bulbs of various shapes and sizes.

Only after I returned home with my trophy did I realize my error.

In France, the base of a bulb is called a *culot*, a word derived from *cul*, which translates as "ass." Although ungentlemanly in some contexts, *cul* raises no eyebrows in others. In polite company, you can refer to the bottom of a bottle as a *cul de bouteille*, or to a dead-end street as a *cul-de-sac*. You can even mention that a woman has a *bouche en cul de poule*, and even though you've just said her mouth resembles a chicken's anus, it's somehow a compliment. *Culot* is similarly inoffensive. The hint at anatomy lies—or perhaps sits—dormant.

Your standard light bulb in France is available in two different asses—the threaded type so common in the US, or the unthreaded model, where two pins stick out like the bolts on Frankenstein's neck. At the store, I'd mistakenly purchased the Frankenstein-type ass, whereas my lamp required the screw-type variety.

Back home the solution would be straightforward: you would exchange the thing. After all, in the US of A the customer is always king. In France, though, it's best to remember

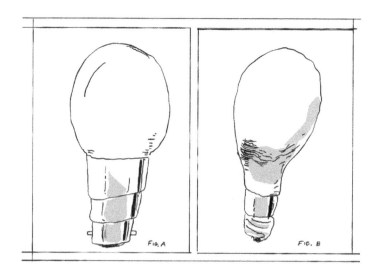

Fig. A   Fig. B

how royals occasionally wind up with their head in a basket. You should expect a little roughing up.

At the store's service counter, I found a middle-aged man with hooded eyes. He was trying to sleep while standing up.

"I'd like to exchange this bulb," I announced.

He struggled to focus. "What's the matter with it?"

"It's the wrong ass." I pointed to the Frankenstein pins. "I need the screw-type."

There was a long silence.

"You can't exchange it here," he said. "You'll need to do it at the register." He seemed rather pleased with himself.

Nothing if not obedient, I navigated through the aisles, pausing to pick up the screw-ass bulb I needed. Soon I had joined the line at the checkout. Because the register I'd selected gives right of way to pregnant women and invalids, both of whom are abundant in my neighborhood, I had time to reflect.

In the States, returning merchandise is not just easy, it is a birthright. Exchanging a purchased article for a different color or size is pretty much expected. Since you can always trade things in later, Americans don't even try to get it right the first time. Usually you can choose to swap your goods for a different product altogether, or even reverse the transaction, backing out as boldly as you might, say, from the Paris Accords or NATO. If there are limits to this principle, I have not encountered them. My mother recently returned a set of dishes despite having used them for five years. Even though she possessed no sales slip or original packaging, and the store could find no record of the sale, they issued her a full refund.

Only later did she happen upon the missing receipt; turns out she'd purchased the stuff elsewhere.

So it goes.

Back at the grocery store it was my turn at the register. The cashier was a large woman shaped much like a pyramid, and nearly as expressionless. I produced the bulb, along with its receipt.

"What's that?" she said.

"I need to exchange it. It has the wrong ass." I held up the screw-ass version I wished to replace it with.

She sat motionless. People behind me were getting antsy. At any moment a pregnant invalid might show up and butt in.

"You can't do that here," she said finally. "You'll have to take it to the service counter."

As a kid I'd found myself in more games of keep-away than I care to admit, so I saw how this would unfold. They'd send me back and forth till I ran home in tears. "I have already been to the service counter," I declared. "They sent me to you."

The Pyramid gritted her teeth. Behind her darkening brow, steam collected.

"Saïd!" she bellowed. "Saïd!"

The man with hooded eyes lumbered forward, and a discussion ensued. Two other cashiers joined the fun. What to do? Was such an exchange allowed? How was it to be handled? Who was authorized to reverse a charge? None of the employees had ever done it before. I traveled from register to register as various cashiers took a run at this feat, the way Olympic hopefuls try again and again to land a triple axel. Eventually a manager was found. He straightened his cuffs, and after twenty minutes of negotiation, a swap was arranged between two bulbs of equal wattage and value.

On my way home, I pondered my lesson. In the States, if you don't like one light bulb, you trade it in for another—as easily as if it were a car, a spouse, or a pair of socks. In France, no matter what bed you've made for yourself, they expect you to lie in it. Whether you're talking education, careers, friends, or home accessories, there are few takebacks. Today's small adventure had revealed the cornerstone of life in France, its base, its very *cul*.

By then I had returned, and I screwed my trophy into the lamp. With a flourish of satisfaction, I flicked the switch. Twice. Three times.

A brief inspection revealed the cause of all my ills: I'd left the cord unplugged after moving the furniture. I didn't need that bulb after all!

I considered returning it.

The Immigrant

AFTER A FEW MONTHS in the thirteenth arrondissement we'd settled into a routine. After breakfast, our daughter would trudge off to middle school, wearing the set jaw of a soldier headed for the front. Anne greeted the day by forcing a pill down the cat's throat. As for me, I confronted the unshaven vagrant who lived in our bathroom mirror, the one whose bed-head hairdo looked like a swirlie from the Ghost of Elementary School Past.

The doorbell interrupted one such moment of self-reckoning, requiring me to pull my jeans over my PJs and scramble down three flights of stairs to the building entrance.

The unexpected caller was a small man with tired eyes and a large mole on his cheek. He wore a navy-blue uniform, the pant legs bunched at the ankles of his black boots. Metal peaked through the straps of a holster, and some kind of whipping stick dangled from his belt. According to the label on his breast pocket, he belonged to the police.

"Monsieur Carpenter?" he said, the mole dancing up and down.

I nodded.

His epaulettes sank as though he'd been hoping for a different answer. "Brigadier Devaux," he said wearily. "I'm afraid I need to ask you to come along with me."

I'd heard lines like this on so many TV shows that I already knew how the rest would unfold: halfway to the station I'd make a break for it, and when I failed to halt, a shot would ring out. My hands would fly up in surprise, and I would crumple to the ground, blood burbling through the hole in my shirt.

My only question was, what crime were they finally hauling me in for?

"I don't know why they're making me do this," Brigadier Devaux said, "but it seems there's a visa problem."

I frowned. Had I gone over my credit limit or something?

But no, he meant the other kind.

More often than not, I enjoy it when things go wrong. Most people don't get to visit the crannies of the world dedicated to fixing problems, but in France I always volunteer to accompany my friends or students to the hospital or dentist. I tag along to help them replace stolen passports or find a locksmith. That way, I get to visit things like hyperbaric chambers, or I learn how to drill out the cylinder of a door lock.

For once, though, I was no mere spectator, and it turns out such scenes are even more compelling when you play one of the principal roles. It would be one thing if I were innocent. Then I'd know it was just a matter of time before Brigadier Devaux and I cleared up the misunderstanding, chuckling away the inconvenience. But a kind of heaviness settled on me—the pall of guilt. Because, in fact, my visa was not entirely in order, where "not entirely" was a euphemism for "not at all," and "not at all" a euphemism for "I didn't even have one."

The brigadier waited downstairs while I fetched my shoes and ran a comb through my hair. At my desk I stuffed a few papers into a bag, along with my checkbook. Who knows? Maybe there would be a fine—or better, a bribe. Since our daughter was at school, she didn't have to watch her father during his last moments of freedom, but Anne looked up from the litter box she was cleaning and asked where I was going.

"I'll be right back," I said. "I have a quick errand to run."

Part of me chalked up this act of lying to stoic heroism—the desire to appear tough and unflappable. But I'm pretty sure it was magical thinking, the way toddlers believe you can't see them when they close their eyes. As long as I downplayed the seriousness of the situation, it would not *be* serious. In fact, who could say? Maybe when I got back down the stairs, Brigadier Devaux would have vanished!

Alas, he had not.

We walked in the direction of the police station, and though I'm usually skilled at chit-chat, words somehow failed me. I'd half-expected the brigadier to cuff me, and when he didn't, I became self-conscious about my hands. Do you let them swing at your sides, or stuff them in your pockets? What was to stop me from poking at Brigadier Devaux's nightstick or revolver? Hands—in fact, arms in general—felt problematic.

I considered the tack I might take during the interrogation, the story I would stick to, as long as things didn't get too rough. The truth was that we planned to stay in France all year, whereas any visit longer than 90 days required a long-stay visa. I had actually attempted to secure one of these precious documents from the French consulate back in the States, but the procedure was so torturous that I'd given up in despair. In the time-honored way of interlopers everywhere, I'd resolved to arrive as a tourist and then simply vanish. I'd done this several times in the past, and usually it was easy. Unless you have the word ILLÉGAL tattooed on your forehead (the more correct word would be CLANDESTIN, but who has enough forehead for that?), no one knows what you're up to. Your outsiderness doesn't announce itself.

So far we'd only been back in Paris for a couple of months, so we hadn't yet overstayed our welcome. But Brigadier Devaux had inexplicably guessed that we *would soon do so*. How, I wondered, had he made that inductive leap, especially when he'd never seen us before? This was a puzzle.

En route the brigadier and I passed the school where my daughter was currently undergoing education. Enrolling her there had been complicated—the kind of labor that would have made Hercules blanch. In the States, you can change schools as easily as your jacket, but in France, it is a cherished opportunity for paperwork. Enrollment is completed at the school itself, but only after an Authorizing Certificate has been issued by the city hall of your arrondissement. I remembered that step well: shortly after our arrival, a desiccated woman at the public services counter had refused my daughter's application. She demanded certain documents, and deemed our excuse for not having them—namely, their non-existence in the US—to be flimsy, refusing to issue the Authorizing Certificate. When I protested, her eyes had narrowed, her lips puckering into a little anus, and suddenly I'd understood. To the mind of this civil servant, I wasn't one of those American tourists riding the fun-train of Paris, dollars tumbling from my pockets. I was, instead, a parasite. She saw me for the larva I was—an immigrant tapeworm ready to slip into the digestive tract of the educational system, where I'd attach to the tissue, glutting myself on the rich fat of Frenchness. Worse, we'd be a whole family of tapeworms, teeming inside the gut of the nation.

Perhaps she was watching us now in her crystal ball as Brigadier Devaux frog-marched me toward justice. How her lips would tighten with satisfaction!

The police station, known locally as the *commissariat*, was a large cube of a building with a broken metal detector. They waved us through cheerily, and I followed Brigadier

Devaux through a labyrinth of desks. Forty or fifty officers milled about, some typing, others on the phone, a few speaking to citizens who resembled normal people but were almost certainly hardened criminals.

It was around this time that I began to regret my stoic leave-taking with Anne. It's easy to be brave in the abstract, but when you're surrounded by uniformed men with firearms, and you know you're in the wrong, it's tempting to wonder if you should have lived your life differently—at least the small part that landed you here.

The brigadier settled me in a chair before his desk, and while he spoke, I took in the surroundings. Over his shoulder a clock was visible on the distant wall, its long second hand jerking through its arc. Two of the fluorescent tubes overhead had burned out. A poster had been ripped from the gray wall, leaving only taped corners behind. It all looked so *real*—the kind of things you'd see in an actual police station. A few desks away an officer conversed with—or, come to think of it, *interrogated*—another man. This fellow was skinny, with curly hair and olive skin. His right leg jiggled nervously, and when he glanced in my direction, I bobbed my head to communicate solidarity.

My attention snapped back to find Brigadier Devaux waiting, the mole on his cheek impatient. What, he wanted to know, was I doing in France? Who was paying my salary?

Anyone who has explained a sabbatical year to an officer of the law knows how shady the whole deal sounds. After all, you receive payments every month for doing pretty much nothing. It smacks of money-laundering, or suggests you've come into possession of compromising photos of your college president. The more Brigadier Devaux squinted, the faster I found myself speaking. Soon my voice warbled worse than during the battle for my daughter's Authorizing Certificate.

Ah, that certificate. At least back then I'd won my case at city hall—finally managing to go over the witch's head. When her supervisor insisted that she process my request, she'd grumblingly stamped the forms, filed the paperwork, and photocopied my passport—the same passport, in fact, that Brigadier Devaux now requested. People were always asking for this document—at the bank or the post office, at the library or the train station. Sometimes it seemed I couldn't order a baguette without producing it.

He studied the blue booklet of my identity, leafing through the pages, and frowning with concentration, the mole on his cheek turning more sinister. Then he folded it closed. "You have no visa," he sighed. He clasped his hands and waited for an explanation.

There's no ideal time to be an illegal alien, but this was an especially bad one. Migrants and refugees were flowing into the European Union. On the edges of French cities, Roma gypsies bivouacked at highway underpasses. Outside Calais a migrant encampment of tents and cardboard had gone up, known as The Jungle. Cardboard lean-tos and tents had pocked the less touristy neighborhoods of the capital.

"Well?" the brigadier asked again. His fingers drummed on the cover of my passport. The future was closing in. Soon I'd find myself in one of those French courts—the kind with walnut-paneled walls and a row of wigged judges glaring down at the witness stand. I would swear on the Bible—though here they probably used some other book people lied about having read, maybe something by Proust—before spilling my guts.

"You'll notice," I said to the unhappy brigadier, "that we've not been here ninety days. So technically a visa isn't required."

"Technically?" he said.

"Technically."

"In that case, might I see your return tickets?"

I fumbled in my bag, hoping they'd gone missing. But no, the damn printout leapt to my fingers. He would now see that our exit from the country wasn't scheduled for another eight months—a direct violation of half a dozen international treaties. In short, my passport showed that I had not *yet* broken the law, whereas the tickets demonstrated that I was *about* to.

I considered surrendering. I would turn over my shoelaces and belt to Brigadier Devaux, and he could lead me directly to prison. Maybe I'd end up in the dungeons of the Chateau d'If—where the Count of Monte Cristo had languished. Or else Devil's Island, or Fresnes, or one of those other locations where daring escapes were the order of the day.

While Brigadier Devaux studied the tickets, I swept my hand across my brow, only to find moisture on my fingers.

What on earth was that doing there? A metallic taste tickled the sides of my tongue, and my stomach hurt. I tried to place the feeling. Then I remembered. This wasn't just uneasiness or the heebie-jeebies. It was actual *fear*—a dread of the future. The sensation felt old and rusty.

All at once the fictional prisons and TV dramas drained from my imagination, replaced by actual courts and holding cells—places with no obligation for a quick narrative resolution.

The brigadier had found a date and marked it with his ballpoint pen. He moved on to page two.

How stupid I'd been! I'd allowed myself shortcuts, assuming that nothing terrible would happen in my future simply because nothing terrible had happened in my past. Like primitive man I'd begun to assume I was immortal simply because I kept waking up each morning.

It got worse. Because of me, Anne was here illegally, too. And what about our daughter? I pictured officers showing up at her middle school at that very moment. She'd have to hold her hands out straight so the cuffs wouldn't fall off her slender wrists. As they led her away, the teacher would nod grimly, her suspicions confirmed.

There was also the damned cat. To keep our daughter happy, we'd decided to bring her pet, and let's just say that *its* papers weren't entirely in order either. The paperwork was confusing, and in the end, I'd drugged the cat till its tongue lolled, before stuffing it in a carrier. Upon arrival I'd snuck the animal past three customs officers engaged in an argument about a soccer match.

What would become of the cat now? Was there a slammer for renegade pets? While we served out our time in the Big House, would the cat join a cell with poker-playing dogs, hard-drinking ones with cigars in their mouths? There was no way this ended well.

The brigadier slid the printout back across his desk, the incriminating evidence circled with blue ink. "I'm really sorry, Monsieur Carpenter," he said. "I wish I didn't have to bother you with this. Frankly, I have more important things to do."

It was the second time he'd apologized for bringing me in. But then, where had it all come from? In France it's possible for the police to stop you anywhere and demand your "papers." It happens a lot in some areas—especially the northern *banlieues*, where undocumented immigrants tend to flock. But in central Paris such requests tend to focus on people selling bracelets on the sidewalk, playing the accordion in the Metro, or picking pockets by the Eiffel Tower. This was a first for me. For better or worse, if you're American, over the age of twenty-one, not entirely broke, sober, in the right part of town, and as lily-white as I am, identity checks are unheard of—the unfairness of which conveyed a karmic quality on the current situation. I definitely had it coming, whatever "it" ended up being.

"Monsieur Carpenter?" he said.

But how had fate pulled it off? Brigadier Devaux hadn't caught me in the middle of a heinous crime. There'd been no dragnet, with detectives reeling in snitches and roughing up lowlifes. No, the officer had simply made a house call. He knew where I lived.

Which could only mean one thing: *someone had tipped him off.*

There's little worse in life than feeling you've been denounced. The world turns gray with suspicion. But not even our friends knew about our visa-less-ness. Which meant that obscure powers had been marshaled against me, a force that was deep and evil, endowed with time, means, and subtlety. I replayed the film of the weeks since our arrival, fast-forwarding through the taxis and the shopping, slowing it at visits to the bank or post office. It had to be someone who had seen my passport, who understood all the rules, and who even knew my address.

In a flash, it came to me.

Back at City Hall, after the supervisor overruled her objections, the pythoness of Authorizing Certificates had stamped my forms. Then she'd taken my passport, opening it to the signature page and flattening it on the copier. And once that was done? Yes, that's when she would have paused. That was the moment when the idea glimmered and the smirk grew on her lips. Shielding her actions with her body, she made another copy, and another—turning the pages of the passport one by one until the record was complete.

That night, after her dinner of toads and newts, she would have hunched over her handiwork at the kitchen table. With a magnifying glass, she'd have deciphered each of the stamps, scrutinizing the dates. How she must have cackled upon the discovery of my imminent infraction. A rule! A rule! And with this, the great sea of bile overflowed, oozing through administrative channels, trickling down the chain of command, until one concentrated green drop landed on the desk of a poor police officer.

"Monsieur Carpenter? Monsieur Carpenter?"

Brigadier Devaux came back into focus. He was leaning even farther over the desk, concern in his eyes.

Why had she gone to such trouble? What made me so undesirable? The answer was simple: I was an outsider, and she was determined to keep it that way. Brick by administrative brick, she had helped to build a wall.

I cast about for an idea, and miraculously one came to me. "Here's the thing," I said to Brigadier Devaux. "The visa is still *in process.*"

Neither of us blinked.

He was no lawyer, so perhaps he wouldn't know you can only obtain a visa while in your home country. Moreover, it sounded plausible. After all, in France, where bureaucracy was quite literally invented, the attention to minutiae means that little gets done on time. It's a longstanding tradition. During the Revolution, for example, stays of execution often arrived after a person's head had been removed. Procedures were procedures, after all.

"Don't worry," I said. "We'll have it all sorted out well before the ninety days are up."

I'm pretty sure we both knew that last part was a lie. But relief had spread across Brigadier Devaux's face. He'd been ordered to investigate an infraction, and I'd just demonstrated there wasn't one.

He stood up. I was free to go!

Then began a delicate negotiation. Was the matter closed, or would I need to come back at the end of my ninety days?

"Well," he said. "Technically, you should."

"Technically?"

He paused. "Yes, technically."

We held each other's gaze, tuning the dials of our brains, each hoping to catch the other man's frequency. Was he telling me not to come back? Would my file be shelved?

"So..." I said, "should I set up an appointment or something...?"

"Oh, I don't think that's necessary. Why don't we...wait and see how it goes."

"Technically?" I said.

"Technically."

I decided against bringing up the cat. Instead, I gathered my documents and bid Brigadier Devaux adieu, retreating through the maze of desks, reining in the impulse to run.

Outside, I blinked in the sunlight. The sidewalks churned with pedestrians, a medley of colors and languages. My steps were light. Life had never smelled fresher. I'd be home before school let out.

As I staggered onward, Devil's Island receded in the mist, along with the walnut-paneled courtroom, the tribunal of judges, my witch-fingered accuser. Just a residue remained, a sticky film over the surface of the present, a reminder of what might have been, what might yet be—or even, for so many other people on Brigadier Devaux's list, what already was.

The Tab

(Or: How to Get in Trouble Without Really Trying)

I adjusted my chair on the terrace of the café to get the sun's full effect. Beer foam tickled my upper lip. More than luxury, it was perfect contentment. Before me paraded the spectacle of the capital. Women strode by with dogs on leashes, vigorous young firemen jogged in formation, tourists studied maps. In the middle of the square, a young couple had stopped to embrace. It was the theater of life, offered for free.

Or almost. The waiter dropped off a plastic saucer with my bill. I patted at my pocket for my wallet, and the universe suddenly contracted.

In my eagerness to peel myself down to nothing, to bask like a lizard on a rock, I'd forgotten the thing that matters most in the City of Light: money.

From my trousers I fished out a paperclip, a crumpled shopping list, and a Metro ticket—not quite enough to cover my debt. The choice of beer now seemed extravagant. Although, when you have no money at all, everything is equally out of reach. I should have ordered champagne!

I thought to phone for help. I needed a lifeline. I'd call Anne at home. And if she wasn't there, I'd go through my list of friends, one after the other, until someone agreed to traipse across town and help me out.

Then I realized my double nakedness. I'd forgotten my phone.

What on earth had I done?

Suddenly the scene playing out on the street took on an odd hue. The men, the women, the tourists, the lovers—they belonged to a different world, the planet of cash. These were people for whom a euro meant nothing or—if such a thing were possible—*even less than nothing*. Whereas, me? I scanned the ground for lost coins, suddenly willing to grovel like those men at the grocery store—the unshaven ones with baggy pants, who always stood before me in line at the cashier, two cans of beer on the conveyor, and a fistful of centimes extracted from passersby.

Now it was I who would become the spectacle. There'd be demands, leading to a confrontation. Perhaps the police would be called. And what if someone I knew saw it go down? Would it make the headlines? Would there be footage on the nightly news? It would probably end up on the internet, where public humiliations are eternal, the way they used to brand the letters *TF* on a convict's shoulder, the indelible mark of guilt, indicating the forced labor—*travaux forcés*—to which he was condemned.

In the Midwest there's a tradition known as the "Dine-and-Dash"—a special form of eating and running reserved for just this kind of occasion. Alas, I feared the custom might translate poorly, landing me once again in the company of Brigadier Devaux.

At the table next to me a couple speaking in Russian prepared to leave. The husband spilled some change onto the saucer to cover his bill, and the coins sparkled in the sunlight. Chairs scooted, and they wandered off. Who would notice if I…? But then the waiter swooped in and collected his due.

In Paris cafés, for the price of a drink you get an unlimited lease on your chair. People nurse coffees for an hour or two or three, and no one will ask you to clear out to make room for others. My emerging plan was to remain at the table till closing—probably seven or eight hours from now—at which point…well, something else would happen. I preferred not to think about it, rather like death.

A phrase sounded behind me. "*Je peux vous encaisser?*" The second waiter had approached one of his tables and asked to cash them out. He was finishing his shift, and although the customers were free to stay, they needed to settle up now.

The back of my neck tingled. How long before my own waiter followed suit?

Money! I'd never had enough of it, of course, but it had always come through in a pinch. Now, though, I had tumbled across the divide, joining the humbling, humiliating side of the have-nots. It turns out there isn't always a Plan B or a Plan C. Sometimes the alphabet just peters out.

I contemplated my possible fates. Washing dishes, if I was lucky. Or perhaps there'd be a scuffle. I'd make a run for it, and a shot would ring out. Back in the States, my mom would get the call inviting her to collect my body. Her lips pursed, she would nod, unsurprised.

But then, a miracle. Across the square, a familiar face flashed. From the sea of unknowns, in this neighborhood I never visited, an acquaintance had emerged. It was

Laurent—someone I actually knew, with whom I was vaguely friendly. He spotted me, waved, walked over. I pumped his hand, and when he asked if he could join me, I beamed. Of course he could! Why not? What a fine day for it! It was like one of those surprise endings in a Greek drama, with Zeus swooping down from the heavens to set everything right.

Probably I should have done the honest thing, coming clean and explaining to Laurent my predicament. But now that I'd been rescued from a great humiliation, I'd raised my ambition, hoping to avoid even a small one.

As he sipped his beer, we launched into the topics of weather and politics, soon followed by trains, firemen, dogs, and finally weekend plans. No topic survived for long. Laurent's conversational style reminded me of Zorro. Like the masked avenger under attack, he dispatched each new subject with a single thrust of his verbal sword, sometimes taking out two or even three at a time. Had a chandelier been available, I'm pretty sure he would have swung from it, the better to repel any new onslaught with his spurred boots. In a matter of minutes, our table was littered with the corpses of conversation. A silence settled upon us. This, I realized, was why Laurent and I had never made it past the friendly acquaintance stage.

Worse, he was only halfway through his beer. I'd been hoping he'd order a second, making it more likely he'd pick up the tab. I considered sending a few more foot soldiers into the conversation.

When, finally, his glass was drained, Laurent smacked his lips. His forehead rippled for an instant, as if he just realized he'd left his gas cooker on at home. He gave me a tight-lipped smile.

"Well," he said.

"Right," I replied.

"I suppose…"

"Me too."

But neither of us budged.

In Paris there's a strange ritual about restaurant checks. In the States it's all based on cowboy heritage, a version of The Fastest Gun in the West: someone whips out a credit card, and the shot is fired. Here, the model is the Phoney War, the strange half-skirmishes between Germany and France in '39. Maybe someone's making a move, but maybe not. It can go on for quite a while.

Laurent sat with his hands folded, his smile somehow wooden. I allowed myself to settle back in my chair, taking in the evening light, fashioning my lips into a grin of contentment. Oh yes, I was prepared to enjoy the surroundings until the End of Time!

It was the waiter who interrupted our stalemate, appearing with his billfold in hand.

"*Je peux vous encaisser?*"

We beamed at each other through gritted teeth. Finally Laurent leaned forward and whispered his request. Would I mind terribly picking this one up? He'd left his wallet at home.

————

In the end, I played the hostage while Laurent trotted to his apartment for our bail. Which gave me time to think—not just about my own fate, but about Fate in general. You can see how it'll go down. The pearly gates will be staffed by a grim waiter with a bad comb-over. He'll be tallying up our deeds, demanding to cash us out. And when we dig through our pockets, won't we all come up a little short? Today's experience was nothing less than a down payment on my day of reckoning.

However, now that I'd been rescued, that shiver of imminent loss was draining away, like a dream after you wake. A fly had drowned at the bottom of my glass, and a chill was settling in the air. Already the world felt distinctly less allegorical.

I checked my watch. Where the hell was Laurent?

The General Assembly

"MAIS NON!" DANIELLE CRIED OUT. Her finger daggered into the air. "That is *inadmissible!*"

Hélène had just brought up the issue of the *déjections canines*—the tidy dog turds people had been finding in the hallways. It was one of many things Danielle found to be beyond the pale. The French word *inadmissible* suggested something unendurable, a hanging offense in the court of human behavior.

"You know who that dog belongs to, right?" Cyril said through his hyena grin. "*La dame du cinquième.*"

Danielle stiffened in her chair and issued a snort. *La dame du cinquième!* The woman on the fifth floor had racked up a long list of infractions, each more egregious than the last.

"I found one too," I offered, eager to join in. Also, it was true. I'd gone out my door the other day, and there in the hallway, at the top of the stairs, lay a brown curlicue. After picking it up in a paper towel, I carried it around for a while, not sure where to put it. The toilet seemed too human. The trash? But no, I didn't want it with me in the kitchen.

Hélène's eyes were cold and owl-like. "We could issue a warning."

Cyril ran his hand over his baldness. "She'll ignore it, just like when her boxes started overflowing into the hallway."

"I took those things," Danielle snapped, "and locked them in the basement. Just wait till she asks for the key!" Danielle was retired, so she had more time than the rest of us for policing our kingdom.

"OK," Cyril said, "We'll add *déjections canines* to the agenda."

It went under Questions of Interest Concerning Life in the Building.

"What about the doorbell—the person who stole it?"

"Who knows? I guess we'll—"

We froze. The floor had creaked outside Hélène's apartment, where our little cabal had gathered. A footstep! Words trembled on our lips. A moment later another creak sounded, this time farther away. We began to breathe again.

And in France, to breathe is to gripe.

I'd been in Paris some months by then, and joining the condo association board seemed the right thing to do—a way of helping out, sharing the load. Besides, Anne and I needed permission for some work we wanted to have done in our apartment. The ancient couple next door had expired (not our fault, I hasten to add; the only blunt instrument involved was time), and by joining their tiny lodging to ours we could offer our daughter what she wanted most: a bedroom. For this to occur, a wall would have to come down, and someone needed to shepherd our request through the process.

"Be honest," Anne told me. "You like the drama."

Which was also true. The fact is, life in France is a closed box, and it's hard to see inside, even if you're as nosy as I am. In our building of some fifty apartments, the people we knew best were the Portuguese concierge and his wife, Monsieur and Madame Carvalho, with whom we exchanged mutually unintelligible greetings on a weekly basis. The other residents plodded through the hallways, their heads down, shoulders rounded. You never caught a glimpse of anyone's private life, and all the doors were lined with steel, bolted at three points, rather like a vault.

Closed doors are a peculiarity of French living. In the States I know people who have front doors made of glass. Often as not, their living room is an exhibitionist's dream, complete with banks of picture windows, brightly illuminated from the inside. When people have shutters in the US, they tend to be vinyl contraptions snapped onto brackets on each side of a window, and they're non-functioning, like vestigial sixth toes. In Paris the only glass in your front door is a five-millimeter peephole, used to examine visitors before you decide whether to open up or tiptoe away. And windows? People equip them with louvered shutters of painted metal, clamping them closed every night. Even on the eighth floor, because you can never be too careful.

Serving on the association board cracks a building open like a dollhouse. You learn who's making late payments, whose plumbing leaks into which neighbor's living room, and how everyone in the building is engaged in a secret mission to scam everyone else. It is the stuff of melodrama, usually kept behind those bolted doors.

As it happened, doors had been the subject of many of our meetings. Our committee had convened in Hélène's apartment to start planning for the *assemblée générale*, or general assembly, which sounds like a meeting of the United Nations, but is really the annual gathering of co-owners in a building. Our concerns about doors included more than Danielle's sequestration of unwanted belongings in the cellar. There were also the locks we'd put on the decommissioned garbage chute, the hydraulic closer we'd installed on the door to the trash can area, and—most annoyingly of all—the problems we'd had with the two front doors, which hadn't worked properly for months.

This last bit requires explanation. In Paris you access most apartment buildings by typing a secret code into a keypad, which unblocks the latch of the first door. Then you enter an area much like the airlock of the International Space Station. One door closes behind you, and then you enter a code on another panel, which finally grants entry to the building itself. But for months now these doors hadn't latched properly, exposing us to impromptu investigations by passersby—as if Chinese and Russian astronauts were docking at our space station unannounced. And even if the latches had been in working order, the five-digit codes on the keypads hadn't been changed for years.

"There's a problem with the keypad company," Cyril explained.

"What *company?*" Hélène puffed. "It's one guy."

"That's the problem. He retired. And he's the only one who has the master code for the panel."

I raised a finger. "Couldn't we track him down and ask for it?"

The three of them stared, incredulous. Interrupt someone's retirement? What planet was I from?

So now, because a fellow had closed up shop and was busy trout fishing in Normandy, our building would have the same security code until the End of Days.

Thanks to our inability to deal with the door issue, people in the building had begun to register complaints, and our little committee was sinking in the polls faster than the current government. And like the government, it turned out we couldn't really do much. The rules of the condo association tied our hands. The annual budget we managed was packed with long-overdue projects, leaving only a fistful of euros for emergencies. Because the doors hadn't announced their failure in advance, we had no money to fix them. To acquire the funds, we needed the approval of our membership, and to gain this approval, we had to wait for the annual meeting. (The United Nations occasionally calls extraordinary sessions of their general assembly, but here that is inconceivable. If our building were on fire and saving it required a vote of the membership, the item would simply be added to the agenda for the coming year.)

There was another issue before our group, and it too was about doors. Cyril had been leading the charge on this one, probably because of the histrionics involved. In real life Cyril is a theater director, which is ideal training for presiding over a condo association. After all, our members are rather like the stock characters of a Molière comedy, a delightful crew of pedants, scoundrels, and Tartuffes. But now we needed his expertise in set design—the creation of illusion by way of flats and scrims—for something weird had happened to our hallways. According to the blueprints, the upper floors of the building were supposed to be identical. But in reality, some of the public hallways stopped short, as if the doorway at the very end of the corridor had one day taken two large steps forward. This was more than trompe-l'oeil decorating; measurements confirmed it.

I could picture how it happened. One day people in our building had left for work, jolly and insouciant, and when they came back that evening, they did a double take. Something had changed. The public hallway was the same, and yet not the same. You saw the same number of doors, but everything felt smaller. The world seemed to be tightening around you—unless it was you yourself who was growing larger. It was *Alice in Wonderland*, but in real life.

The truth was more mundane. While everyone was at work that day, a group of handymen had knocked free the doorway at the end of the corridor and scooted it forward two meters, reframing the wall around it. *Voilà!* The proud homeowner had expanded his territory. It was ingenious, in a let's-invade-Austria kind of way. And after the first annexation, people on other floors had followed suit.

"And that's not all," Cyril explained. "There are also the balconies."

On the top two floors of our building a few apartments used to have large balconies. These were apparent in the blueprints, too. And yet, when you stood in the street and looked up, the balconies were gone, replaced with strange protuberances in the exterior walls, pocked with windows.

"They've closed them in," Cyril said.

Danielle was outraged. This, too, was *inadmissible*. "They have to undo it," she said.

"It was years ago," Hélène mused unhappily. "There's a statute of limitations."

She was right. For decades now, people had been conquering tidbits of our building during midnight raids as if it were no big deal, as if they didn't need to ask anyone's permission, as if it kind of belonged to them anyway. Except that it didn't! The annexed areas belonged to the whole association, were part of the public spaces. It didn't matter that no one ever stood in those unused bits of hallway; the point was that you could if you wanted to.

It's not surprising that people wanted more room, because in Paris there's not enough to go around. After all, this is one of the most densely populated cities in the world—worse than London or New York or Shanghai. But still. Hallways and balconies? What was next—mailboxes and window ledges? Suddenly I felt more sympathy for *la dame du cinquième*; sure, she'd been spilling into the public space with her boxes and her dog turds, but at least she hadn't framed in new walls.

"Still," Cyril said, "we need to do something. Because of the umpteenths."

And he was right. Time may have silted over the changes, making them impossible to undo. But no one had ever recalculated the measurements.

Umpteenths are the way you divvy up financial obligations in a building. Each apartment comprises a portion of the total surface area—usually some crazy fraction like 312 / 23,916ths. Whenever building expenses arise—Monsieur and Madame Carvalho's salary, for example, or repairs, or heating—a person's share of the cost depends on his or her umpteenths. For years now the rest of the building had covered the cost of heating other peoples' annexed hallways and balconies. Enough was enough!

Except that in France enough is never enough. Because it all happened so long ago, most of those who had encroached on the public space had sold to new owners. The new occupants didn't understand why they should be held to account for the sins of their predecessors. A couple knuckled under, but a few others developed strategies for resistance. One fellow kept playing the simpleton, claiming he didn't understand what it was all about, and he lurched from one annual meeting to the next without ever following through on what the previous year's meeting had told him to do—namely, hire a professional geometer, talk to the notary, etc., etc. He figured we'd give up eventually. But he hadn't reckoned on Danielle, who had the tenacity of a Jehovah's Witness.

The big question now was how to get people to show up for the general assembly. Attendance was always low. Although our members whined about how we managed things, the last thing they wanted was for us to stop managing them. Most of the members preserved their right to complain by boycotting the annual meeting. But this year, we needed them. Adjusting the umpteenths required a super-majority.

How to get an audience: this was another thing Cyril knew about from the theater.

He and I strategized about it one day up on the rooftop, eight stories up. We didn't really need a cone of silence for the discussion, but we had to examine the plumbing stacks anyway, so we shimmied up the ladder and pushed open the skylight. Soon we were standing on the zinc-lined platform of a roof that rounded down at the mansards. Paris was at our feet. In the distance you could even make out that skeletal tower the city is known for.

Neither of us wanted to get too close to the edge. Cyril is pretty slim, and a good puff of wind might carry him off. Luckily, his bald head makes him more aerodynamic.

The silence grew long.

"We're pretty high up," I ventured, although I couldn't bring myself to look over the edge.

"Yep," he concurred. "It's pretty high."

We checked out the plumbing stacks, which were due for an inspection, and as happens when you're chatting about plumbing, this led to a discussion about toilets, since one of the waste lines had recently backed sewage into some of the apartments. We identified most of the stacks, which ran through all the floors. But one was missing.

"What about the Carvalhos' place?" I asked, peering into the black mouth of one of the pipes. The ground floor was anomalous because of the concierge's tiny apartment. I couldn't find a plumbing stack for it.

There was no such stack, Cyril explained, because they didn't have a toilet.

"You mean it's broken?" I said.

"No, no. That's how it's always been."

I blinked three times before the idea settled. The Carvalhos had lived in the building for thirty years—had raised kids here—and they'd only had access to the toilet in the public hallway. That was how the building had been constructed in 1930, and it had never been changed.

I don't get exercised about much, but still. Not having the right to pee in your own house? That was like…well, like the way *la dame du cinquième* treated her dachshund, leaving it to do its business in the hallways.

"But," I sputtered, "That's…that's…*inadmissible!*"

Even Cyril agreed—partly because now we could try to rally the membership via moral indignation. It would attract a few more owners to the meeting.

"Of course," he added, "there's also the radiator issue. That might help."

He was talking about a new law requiring us to meter how much heat went into each apartment. It was sure to be expensive and ineffective, but probably not outrageous enough to propel us to a quorum. No, for that we needed something big. Something looming. Something irresistible.

The idea came when Hélène and I went to the building management company, known as the *syndic*, for the annual review of the accounts. Our contact there is Madame Lesur, a plump woman with bug eyes and quick gestures. Hélène did the heavy lifting as we went through the receipts, entrusting me simply to read out the totals—a poor choice on her part, given my numerical limitations. When we finished, Madame Lesur scooted her chair forward and listened intently as we unfolded our problem. How, we asked, could we get a critical mass at the meeting? Her eyes, apparently not equipped with lids, glistened steadily, and her answer came in a single word: *Ravalement.*

It was a brutal move—like that crusader of old who, unsure which of his prisoners were Christians and which were miscreants, declared they would "kill them all, and let God sort it out." With a single word, Madame Lesur had elevated our general assembly from the register of afternoon TV to that of Verdi and Wagner. This was opera—which, after all, is mostly bickering in a foreign language, set to music.

In France, the word *ravalement* chills the heart and petrifies the pocketbook. It has to do with the upkeep of a building's exterior. The Larousse dictionary makes a *ravalement* sound like a good scrubbing of the building's skin. But in this, as in most things, the lexicon lies. The process is closer to reconstructive surgery—the big kind, where they transplant a whole new face on you after you've been mauled by baboons. The word is sometimes used to refer to other dramatic transformations: some aging beauty will disappear from society, and when she reappears with her jowls tightened and her face swollen with botox, people will whisper that her façade just had a *ravalement*.

But Madame Lesur was right. Our building *was* overdue for a serious facelift. In Paris buildings are supposed to redo their outside every ten years, though that deadline is routinely ignored. In our case we were approaching the seventeen-year mark, and it showed. The stucco on the outside was dingy, crazed with hairline cracks. Worse, the cornices and ledges were surrendering to the elements. One day Madame Carvalho was weeding in the building's garden when a block of concrete thumped to the ground next to her left foot. It had fallen eight stories.

A *ravalement* means constructing Tinkertoy scaffolding from the sidewalk to the rooftop, all the way around the building, and leaving it there for weeks or months. Men in boots stomp by your third-floor window while you're snapping your undies on. The walls shudder so hard during the hammering that wine glasses march off the shelves, row by row, like a herd of lemmings. And if they sandblast, your life ends up quilted in dust. Worst of all, it costs thousands—indeed, hundreds of thousands for a building our size. The vastness of the sum was sure to get people's attention. It certainly got mine. After all, we'd just acquired the apartment next door, which doubled our share. I did a quick estimation of what we'd have to shell out, subtracted the sum from our savings, and ended up with a negative number. If only the neighbors had held on for another year! Dying had been their trick for avoiding the *ravalement*.

I was still a member of the building committee, so technically pro-*ravalement*, but I had definite sympathies with the anti-*ravalement* camp. Should I yield to the common good, or could I justify my natural self-centeredness? Were we all in it together, or was it every man for himself? It was one of those dramatic climaxes—the battle between duty and desire, between paying and getting, between having your cake and eating it.

And it wasn't just me. Opinions were sure to be divided. Some owners always wanted the building to look good. Others experienced physical pain each time they parted with a euro. And some smart aleck was sure to take our headline topics—the toilet and the *ravalement*—and play them off one another, pointing out that if blocks of rubble rained down hard enough on the Carvalhos, the new toilet might not even be necessary.

But one way or the other, people would see the urgency of getting the umpteenths straightened out, because with a *ravalement* looming, you sure didn't want to pay the share owed by somebody else's hallway or balcony.

Our campaign began. The agenda went out to the membership. Cyril, Danielle, Hélène and I started courting the neighbors, reminding them to attend or offering to handle their proxies. We called and emailed. We posted a notice in the elevator. As we went door to door, I crossed paths with the rogue dachshund marauding through the hallways, trying to master his bowels until *la dame du cinquième* got him out for a walk. Maybe we could count the dog toward a quorum?

And then, as in all great dramas, we had a sudden reversal, or at least a change of course. Two weeks before the general assembly one of France's cell phone companies, Bouygues Telecom, sent us a letter. Their customers were complaining about poor coverage in our neighborhood, so Bouygues was on the prowl for a building where they could plant a relay tower. We happened to be in the sweet spot. In exchange for a few meters of rooftop, they'd pay a licensing fee fat with zeros.

At first our committee chattered with elation. Bouygues Telecom was our hero, rising from the shadows like the Phantom of the Opera! But then came a shudder of caution. What if that mask concealed a villainously curled mustache? Sure, the antenna could be our money tree, but wouldn't it also turn the building into a microwave oven, one stuck permanently on defrost? We rushed to the internet. Were cell towers dangerous? Were the safeguards sufficient? The jury was out. Farmers said the signals decreased milk production in cows. City dwellers complained of headaches. One woman claimed to receive phone calls through her dental fillings. We reasoned that the lower floors of the building— where all the members of our committee happened to reside—were probably safe from any damaging rays. As for the upper floors...well, maybe it wasn't so bad that they'd closed in those balconies after all! Maybe now would be a good time for them to wallpaper their ceiling with tinfoil.

We let the membership know about this new twist.

At the general assembly we had a full house. There was a buzz of excitement, like an opening night. Our show was about to begin. The setting was pretty simple—less the elegant decor of Mozart than the artist's garret of *La Bohême*. Finally Madame Lesur strode in, files bundled under her arm. A hush passed over the group as if the conductor had just stepped up to the rostrum. Her bulging eyes swept from left to right, and we held our breath. A binder flipped open and she clicked her pen. The meeting began.

Another way general assemblies remind me of opera is just how darned long they are. Both genres start with a kind of tedious overture that drags on before the real story begins. It takes ages to introduce all the characters. And once the action starts, you plod from scene to scene in a pretty predictable way. People play their parts, repeating the same lines, and sometimes the discussion simply stalls, like those scenes in Verdi where lovers engage in what you might call a Minnesota goodbye—a lot of foot shuffling and throat clearing, followed by ten or twenty renditions of *addio, addio*, before they finally shove off.

As we began our laborious ascent toward a climax, I tinkered with a libretto for the stage version. It went something like this:

CYRIL: And now a new question.

CHORUS: Hush! A new question, a new question.

CYRIL: Shall we install…

CHORUS: Install what? Install what?

CYRIL: Shall we install meters? Meters on every radiator?

CHORUS: Whatever for? Whatever for?

HÉLÈNE: So each shall pay his due.

DANIELLE: Pay his due and nothing more.

CHORUS (PART ONE): But we don't want to pay for this!

CHORUS (PART TWO): We don't want to pay for that!

CHORUS (ALL): We don't want to pay for anything!

MADAME LESUR (rising): It's the law.

CHORUS: But if it's the law, why must we vote?

MADAME LESUR: Because it's the law. You must vote, and you must vote yes!

CHORUS: But we don't want to pay for this! We don't want to pay for that. We don't want to pay for anything!

MADAME LESUR: But you must!

CHORUS: But we won't!

MADAME LESUR: But you must!

CYRIL: The question is called. How do you vote?

CHORUS: Well, if we must…

MADAME LESUR: Yes you must.

CYRIL: The motion passes! The motion passes!

CHORUS: *Addio, addio! Addio, addio, addio!*

I'm still working out some of the metrical kinks. The radiators are just Act One, and the drama climbs when the toilet arrives in Act Two. Act Three—which includes both the cell tower and the umpteenths—is positively Wagnerian, studded with a breathtaking aria on the theme of injustice, sung by *La Dame du Cinquième*.

In the end, we made some headway. The radiators would be metered and the cell tower studied. The Carvalhos would get a toilet. The *ravalement* and our collective impoverishment was put off for another year, although the umpteenths were updated. Anne and I were authorized to open up the wall between our two apartments. And after much grumbling, the membership re-elected our committee for another term of loyal service.

Afterwards, Cyril, Danielle, Hélène, and I had a drink. As the adrenaline of the performance wore off, I dragged myself to bed where I slept hard, my dreams swirling with orchestras and makeup, the crunch of crinoline. When I woke, the sun had burned through the Parisian gray. A hint of summer was in the air. I splashed fresh water on my face and decided to treat myself to a pastry. Hadn't I earned it? And as I opened the door to head down to the bakery, something lay in wait on the floor at the head of the stairs. It was a tidy coil of brown.

PART TWO

Saw

French Like Moi

I HAVE NEVER WATCHED LOCUSTS swarm a field of wheat, but I bet it looks a lot like Paris when the tourists arrive. Each year fifteen million of these creatures descend on the city, stripping the stores and restaurants bare, and since they squeeze their visits into the summer months and the central arrondissements, it's surprising they don't have to stack all the sightseers in human pyramids just to make room.

When the city is this thick with other nationalities, spotting an actual Parisian is something of a rarity, and if he or she happens to be especially endearing—that is, accompanied by a small and smartly dressed child, walking a dog, wearing a scarf, charging across cobblestones on stiletto heels, and/or displaying a look of purposeful exasperation—the appearance can elicit the kinds of oohs and shutter-clicks usually reserved for zoo exhibits of meerkats.

It's a big responsibility for the locals to perform their nationality so relentlessly. Most theatrical actors get to move from one production to another, and if they're unionized they even accrue vacation time. But for Parisians life is like indentured servitude to the Broadway production of *Cats*: you're in it for the long haul. Only when you get home at night can you finally peel off the necktie that's been chafing all day, mess up your hair, pull on the sweat pants, and crack open a beer while the TV warms up to reruns of *America's Got Talent*. (I've always assumed the French lead secret lives as Americans.)

Because it's such a burden for Parisians to keep the ball of Frenchness rolling, I sometimes chip in and give it a push, putting my years of cultural imitation to work. For instance, I'll be walking across a bridge as a Bateau Mouche approaches. A gaggle of tourists will crowd the upper deck, their attention split between the Left and Right Banks, fingers pointing at spires and domes, the hum of voices audible above the engines. Meanwhile, a kid—usually a little girl—stands glumly at the front, elbows on the railing, cheeks wedged in the V of her palms. She reminds me of my own daughter—except for the weight of her sadness. Her parents are so busy capturing video footage of debris floating down the Seine that they've forgotten she exists. *No, no, the mom is probably crabbing at the dad, you're in selfie mode. Give it here.* They fidget with the device, prodding with their forefingers. Meanwhile, the girl sighs, and for a brief instant, there's only one person in the entire universe paying attention to her: me, glancing down from the bridge. Then it happens. She lifts her head and sees me seeing her.

We exchange A Look. Slowly she raises her cupped palm to the side of her pageboy hair, and the hand wags back and forth in secret communication. Because I'm still a human being, I stop and wave back, trying to signal not just across the rapidly closing distance between me and the boat, but across the years, the decades. *Don't worry*, I want to tell her. *It gets better.* I give a little nod to convey my sympathy. Yes, her parents are idiots. Her teachers don't understand her. Her best friend has moved away. And even this trip, the family vacation to Europe, designed to bring them all together, and failing utterly, it too will fade to nothing, as will it all—except for this one moment, the few seconds during which she found understanding in the small wave of a man's hand before her boat disappeared under a bridge in Paris.

Then one of the grownups, probably the dad, notices the girl and her raised hand. His face rotates in my direction, his nose pulling into a rabbit scrunch as he searches for the target of her attention. He spots me, my hand frozen in place. And I think, *uh-oh*.

In the States, it's worrisome when a grown man waves to a little girl in secret. I figured the parents' thoughts would jump to *Lolita*. And because during their boat tour they'd have learned about the Conciergerie—the place where Marie Antoinette spent her last days—they would take me there now so I could await execution, or castration, or whatever happened to be the punishment *du jour*.

But no! Instead, the dad's hand has gone into the air, too. He's…waving. Then the mom turns and sees. She kneels by her daughter's side and beams up at me, her hand sweeping back and forth. Now others turn and notice. The boat is so close I can make out the color of their eyes. And suddenly all the paws are in motion, as if a platoon of Chinese Lucky Cat figurines were bearing down on me.

Already the photos would be trickling onto Facebook— pictures of me with this caption: *Friendly Parisian.*

In this manner I sometimes play a local for the benefit of tourists. It's a public service I provide to lighten the load for my neighbors. The fact that I don't look the least bit French doesn't seem to be an obstacle. Maybe the wicker basket I carry to the market distracts from my height, or the Lacoste jacket obscures the Germanic blandness of my face. I used to wonder if time in Paris would make me more French on the outside—the way scientists before Darwin thought antelopes would become giraffes if they strained for leaves long enough. But no, my face hasn't narrowed and my cheekbones haven't budged. The only indigenous feature I display is an ability to stroll without the company of a flag-toting guide, or, indeed, anyone. After all, tourists don't travel alone. They know what separation from the herd means: the local jackals will circle, ribbons of saliva hanging from their fangs. Me, I just mingle with the jackals.

There's also the fact that I'm pretty oblivious to the world around me, which can sometimes be mistaken for the studied aloofness of Parisians. Tourists specialize in gaping—not only at the Eiffel Tower and the Arc de Triomphe, but even at racks of Vélib bicycles or offerings in bakery windows. For them, a child zipping to school on a kick scooter is worth a thousand Louvres.

Parisians, as a rule, ignore it all. One day I walked down a street to find an African lion approaching from the other direction. The animal was proud and fierce, poised mid-growl on a spit of rock that left him a head taller than the Parisians he rumbled past. Two women pulled him on a dolly. When the animal and its handlers halted at an intersection, I couldn't help thinking the beast was waiting for the light, as though the little man had to turn green before the lion would be allowed to choose one of us for eating.

It's true the great cat was stuffed, destined for the natural history museum, but still, none of the passersby had batted an eye. Turning their head might muss their *foulard*, so they plodded forward in their world-weary way, as though lions were no more surprising in Paris than squirrels in the Midwest.

In the midst of this menagerie, I've become one of the exhibits for the tourists—one more meerkat disappearing into the burrows of the Metro. Often visitors are content to view me passing, or watch me looming over them from a bridge. On other occasions, however, they embolden themselves to approach the native-like fauna. The people I encounter fall into four different categories:

CATEGORY ONE: THE FRENCH. Natives who have lost their way often stop me for directions, but as soon as they detect my accent, their smile stiffens and their ears close. Although I've lived in the neighborhood for a long time and actually frequent the very florist they are trying to locate—her shop is on the ground floor of the building I live in—my answer to them is useless because by definition I cannot know anything.

CATEGORY TWO: THE GENERIC FOREIGNER. Someone—let's say an Italian—asks me for information in halting French. In such a case, because my knowledge of the visitor's native language is limited to different shapes of pasta, I respond in French, our common tongue, and I part ways satisfied that I have helped another human being.

CATEGORY THREE: THE ANGLOPHONE-ANGLOPHONE. Some English speakers approach me as a last resort, as though they would rather bleed to death or lapse into a hypoglycemic coma than utter a word in another language. You can read the terror in their pupils as they join together words from their phrasebook and brace for the impact of a response. I address such guests to our city politely in English, watching their grimace melt into relief. (Once a woman from Alabama commented on how good my English was, and when I explained that I was American, she hesitated. "Well," she said, "it's not *that* good.")

CATEGORY FOUR: THE FRANCOPHONE-ANGLOPHONE. Some American travelers yearn for encounters with otherness. Tired of waiters and shopkeepers who respond in English whenever they attempt to use the local idiom, these tourists hanker for the deeper connection, a skirmish with *authentic Frenchness*. By mistake they sometimes zero in on me, and I find myself delivering laborious responses in French, which I know are only half-understood. When these people wander off in the opposite direction from the one I just indicated, I console myself with the thought that I've provided them with a memory—a small event that they can later burnish into a story, an anecdote about that long conversation Dale or Judy managed to have with *a Parisian*, finally using that language they'd "learned" back in high school.

In this way I trudge about town as a purveyor of authentic experience, rather like those men who lay out rows of suspect Louis Vuitton bags in the subway stations. Authenticity is in the eye of the beholder, I tell myself—though also, in some cases, the eye of the police. My daughter considers my behavior dishonest, but by that definition, I tell her, even Christmas is dishonest. It's true that when I play the

Santa Claus of Frenchness—waving from bridges to Bateau-Mouche-bound children, or helping my countrymen locate the public toilets—I'm doling out gifts that don't, strictly speaking, belong to me. But it's less theft than generosity. I'm not asking for a medal or anything. It's not a huge sacrifice. But still.

It was in this frame of mind that I found myself returning home from the theater one night. It had been a new-fangled performance of *Hamlet*—set, for reasons I didn't understand, in a '70s era British pub with a graffiti-covered men's room and a jukebox that erupted into disco tunes at unexpected moments. Guildenstern was played by a hand puppet shaped like a dog cradled in the crook of Rosencrantz's arm, and

King Claudius had been demoted to a surly pub owner. In this unusual context we watched poor Hamlet—blessedly, from behind—while he peed at the urinal, craning his neck and crying out "To be or not to be" in French: *Être ou ne pas être.*

It was enough to give one pause (or, in the case of the Guildenstern puppet, the appendages that go by the same name). After all, here was a play written in English, where all the characters were supposedly Danish but now somehow spoke French. Strangely, I found myself identifying with them. Wasn't this the kind of performance I engaged in daily—even if, all modesty aside, I generally did a more convincing job of it than this particular effort by the *Comédie-Française?* When they got to the part about the play within the play, performed in silence except for the ABBA tune throbbing in the background, it reminded me of all those pantomimes I'd employed to help foreigners understand the city.

It was thus with a renewed sense of mission that I stepped onto the Metro after the production. It was evening-bustle time, so the car was rather full—your standard mix of theater-goers headed home, young kids just starting to prowl, a drunkard sprawled on a seat, and a jumble of tourists. A man with scruffy dark hair had strung a curtain between two poles at the end of the car, and as we jerked into motion a familiar tune started. A muppet of Luciano Pavarotti—barrel-chested and bearded—appeared over the top of the curtain, and it burst into song, belting out "La donna è mobile" from Verdi's *Rigoletto*.

A minute later the doors opened at another stop, allowing a refueling of passengers. As we started again, I found myself standing next to a family of three. They were American. The scowling man was rather short and square, and I pictured him rolling out from underneath Chevrolets on a mechanic's creeper. His wife stood a bit taller, big-boned, her eyes imprinted with a pained expression. Their son, maybe ten, was a waif of a child—with the dad's red hair and his mother's nose, but narrow-shouldered and delicate—a surprising collision of genes. His mother's hand was clamped about his wrist so as to prevent his abduction by gypsies, while the boy's eyes suggested that he longed for just such an event.

Behind me the miniature Pavarotti ground through his tune, rather like the jukebox I'd been subjected to earlier. In front of me, the parents had turned to squint at the subway map above the door, pointing at stations. Bits of their conversation burbled through the soup of noise.

"No, no," I heard the husband mutter in an irritated tone.

"I think it is," the wife responded, and she pulled out a guidebook, opening it to a map.

A kind of hushed argument ensued about whether they were headed in the right direction, their words twanging in a way that reminded me of Nashville, or maybe rural Kentucky. Then the husband issued a grunt of exasperation—not about the map or the subway or even Paris, but about this wife of his, the one struggling so hard to make everything right. All at once, I didn't like him.

Then the wife's eye caught mine and she stepped forward, asking in severely fractured French if indeed the train was headed for their destination. It was your standard CATEGORY THREE encounter, one where I would ordinarily respond in English. However, invigorated by the French-English-Danishness of *Hamlet*, I believed I could offer her a CATEGORY FOUR response, demonstrating before the eyes of her husband—and more importantly, in front of her son, who tracked this activity with interest—her excellence and moral superiority as a human being skilled in interactions with others.

"*Oui*," I announced. And to underscore this reply, I used my finger to point at the subway map, tracing along the line to the station where they would get off.

Then came a profusion of desperate thanks, uttered in a way that called to mind the long-forgotten connection between *merci* and mercy. I had done a good deed. And to drive it home, I now bestowed a look of sympathy upon their young child. To wave at him here might seem excessive, but I allowed myself a nod. *Yes*, my bowed head said, *it's a difficult stretch, but you'll grow out of it. Your father loves you in his own way. Your mother is trying. And what you don't know now, but that you'll learn one day soon, is that—*

Which is when the dad spoke again.

"Ask 'im about tomorrow," he said, pronouncing it *tamarah*. "How d'we get to the *louver*?"

I gathered he meant the museum. The wife winced. She tried to wring a few more words from the damp cloth of her memory, but the exercise produced physical pain.

When a corner of her husband's mouth rose, I understood immediately. He wasn't interested in louvers. He didn't care about museums or sights. All he wanted was to flummox this poor woman, to knock her off the pedestal of the puny success she had accomplished, shoving her back into the dirt.

Behind us the music paused while the Pavarotti muppet mopped his brow with a white handkerchief. He started singing again with renewed energy.

The mother struggled for a long while, but finally her lips parted. A little jumble of French-like sounds tumbled out, a couple of them recognizable.

Having committed myself to CATEGORY FOUR, I had little choice but to forge ahead, albeit with the sense of foreboding that accompanied soldiers leaping from trenches at the Battle of the Somme. I uttered an explanation to her in baby French, separating all my words, decorating each one with a gesture. But the woman's eyes grew small as she strained to understand. She had the pleading look of a beaten dog.

"What'd he say?" the man pressed in a sneering tone. After a pause, he tried again. "What'd he say?"

The train had now stopped at another station, and I was tempted to run, to leave this family to its fate. But I thought again of *Hamlet*—not so much the urinals, but the words. The slings and arrows, the outrageous etc., etc. On stage it had all washed over me in a French version of Danish-English. Wasn't that the way out? It was all a question of performance.

"*Yoo seee,*" I said to the woman in English, harnessing my best caricature of a French accent. "*Fore zee Louvre, yoo goh to zees station.*" And I punctuated it with a poke at the subway map.

It was the perfect solution. Neither CATEGORY THREE nor CATEGORY FOUR, but something in between—enough to show the husband that his wife had gotten her point across, and that a willing French person would even step over the linguistic divide for her.

Her face lit up, and I checked to make sure the man's scowl had returned. It wasn't enough for me that heaven should exist for the wife; her husband had to end up in hell.

Behind us, passengers were getting on, and Pavarotti's voice trilled, but I returned my gaze to their little boy, who watched with wonder. I felt honored to be present at such a formative moment—indeed, to have played a role in a scene this boy would reenact on the stage of his imagination as he grew into a teenager, a young man, or even when he had a family of his own, and—

"Yer a meer-kin," a voice said.

It was the husband speaking again, though not to his wife. He was looking directly at me, his nose pulled tight, his thick lips hanging apart.

"Aren't'cha?" he pressed.

Now it was my turn to strain to understand. Exactly what was this little Claudius accusing me of? Could a meer-kin possibly be the baby of a meerkat—a kind of meer-kitten?

I said it again in my head. *Meer-kin.* What was a *meer-kin?* He couldn't possibly mean a "merkin," could he—those medieval masks for one's private parts? Was he accusing me of being a codpiece, a prop?

"Yer a meer-kin," he said again, louder. Heads turned in our direction.

Suddenly I understood.

A tone sounded, and the train doors closed in slow motion.

It was quickly turning into a CATEGORY FIVE situation, rather like a hurricane. Scores of tourists had taken me for a local, but somehow this plain and blunt man, alone among them, had unmasked me, stripping me utterly, leaving not so much as a fig leaf.

The train had rumbled into motion. I smiled at the husband and gave a shrug, imitating a man who doesn't understand. However, since I'd already demonstrated I could speak the language of Shakespeare, that performance felt hollow, and heat rose to my face. The mother's expression had now turned to incredulity, and even the boy's eyes had widened.

Pavarotti had finally completed his aria, and the quiet of the car was interrupted only by the puppeteer making the rounds with his leather purse, asking for coins. The husband glared at me, gearing up to launch another assault.

I looked about, hoping an African lion might suddenly appear to distract us. But no, they're only around when you don't need them.

It's worth noting that Paris has one of the world's oldest subways. The first line of the *Métropolitain* opened in 1900 on the occasion of a World's Fair, and with over a century of experience, the transit authority has learned to provide for every imaginable situation, including warnings about the danger of pinched fingers and instructions about who is authorized to sit where. To the left of each door, just above the window, a thick red handle is affixed. It is the emergency brake. Pull it down, and the entire train will shudder to a stop. Over the years I have often wished for such a device, not only in public transportation, but at home, in various workplaces, and especially at family gatherings—all those times where you'd like to stop the world so you can get off. Never before had I felt such a deep urge to go for the red handle. One more move on the part of the husband, and I was ready to lunge for it.

Then the puppeteer was there, pressing between us. "*S'il vous plaît*," he begged, pushing the leather purse in our faces. "*S'il vous plaît.*" Cradled in his other arm, wide-eyed Luciano Pavarotti stared at us.

The husband swatted at the air, waving him away, but the man somehow took this as encouragement, turning from one of us to the other, the hand outstretched. "*S'il vous plaît, s'il vous plaît.*"

"Go away," the husband snarled. He turned back to me.

But then a coin glinted. It was the boy. He had pulled a euro from his pocket—almost certainly his entire fortune—and ignoring his father's protests, he deposited this treasure in the man's purse. The puppeteer gave him a deep bow, and in thanks he swung his muppet forward, clicking the music on. Pavarotti began a jolly new tune of thanks, a melody over which it was impossible to speak.

The train creaked to a stop at the next station, and the doors opened. I leapt to freedom. And as the tone sounded, I turned, exchanging a look with the child who had paid my ransom. He raised his hand in a small wave, and in his eyes I understood it all. *I'm sorry*, his look said. *You're a grown-up, and that's not easy. The situation is bad and getting worse. Your daughter is growing up and your wife knits. The unknown has vanished. You are burdened with understanding.*

But don't worry, said his eyes. *It won't go on forever.*

The Acute and the Grave

"So," MY FRIEND SABINE ASKED, "what city do you fly into?"

I was headed for the States, with a first port of call on the eastern seaboard. "Newark," I replied—although, because we were speaking in French, I didn't really say "Newark," but instead replaced that clipped little name with the stretched-limousine French version, separating the vowels and turning the metropolis of belching smokestacks into something suddenly svelte: "*Nou-ark.*"

Sabine pulled a look, one eyebrow rising as the other dipped. Was it possible she'd never heard of it? I clarified where the place was located: "*Nou-jair-ssay.*"

Her eyes rolled toward the heavens. "*Mon dieu.* I suppose you think that's clever."

She was talking, of all things, about my accent—or rather, about my pretending not to have one. I am, for better or worse, an American, so what business did I have pronouncing words like "Newark" and "New Jersey" *à la française*? Such names were among the few things I was expected to utter correctly—which is to say, like the Yank I am.

I managed a pinched smile, but in the little diary I keep tucked in the back of my brain, I took note. *See? You can't win.* Most of the time, if you plop an American name or word into a conversation without churning it through the mill of French pronunciation, nobody knows what you're talking about. I noticed this long ago, back during the George Bush presidency. Hapless but well-intentioned Americans faltered in French conversations having to do with Dubya. In the American version, the u in Bush is so relaxed it has practically gone on vacation, whereas French makes you choose between stark alternatives, turning this man of state into a homonym for *bouche* ("mouth") or *bûche* ("log," or, in slang, "blockhead"). Despite the temptation of the second option, it's the first that gained currency. Nevertheless, lots of Americans opted for a third option—that is, doing what Sabine had told me to do with New Jersey, blurting the thing out in American. But if you do that, French people tend to squint and wrinkle their nose. They are lost. Saying "bush" instead of *bouche* or *bûche* is like shifting a beehive six inches while the drones are out: the poor critters never make it home again.

French people have it easy, for they routinely Frenchify American words. Americans, though, are stuck. We're supposed to convert American names into French, except when our conversation partner prides himself on his English. In that case we're expected to yokel it out with exaggerated Americanness.

At least most of the time. A little experimentation reveals that the American accent you employ has to be in line with the colorless tones of network news anchors—pretty much what you'd find in central Nebraska. Try dropping *Nawlins* or *Loosiana*—or, for that matter, *New Joy-zee*—into your French, and even the sticklers will start to back down.

It's hard to know how far to take this. Some cases are easy. For instance, after decades of brainwashing by imported crime series, the French have learned to refer to our Federal Bureau of Investigation as the *Eff-Bee-Eye*, and only the most overzealous American would attempt to twist it back to the French letters, *Eff-Bay-Ee*. But what about the ends of those shows, when the crime has been solved—or, even better, thwarted? Then you're in front of a happy ending—a story-telling concept so foreign that the French have no word for it in their own tongue, therefore referring to it as *le happy end*—beheading the h of happiness when they say it. What then? Are those of us with US passports supposed to twang out *hhhappy end*, inserting an American accent in our French, as if this expression actually existed in English?

Of course, Americo-Parisians (or Pariso-Americans) get to deal with this both coming and going. Stateside I hesitate at the American pronunciation of words like *croissant* or *crêpe*. Depending on the situation, I wonder if I've been deputized to carry the banner of false-Frenchness, or if this is one of those occasions where *croy-sant* and *crayp* are more appropriate. Often the French and English wires cross in my brain, and as sparks fly I utter some monstrous coupling of the two. If I catch myself in time, I simply choose something else from the menu.

The accent business may not be as big as Google or 3M, but there are legions of French teachers in the US, each one training students to gargle their R's and squeak their I's. They make a big deal of it. The idea seems to be that when you travel to a foreign land, you should try to fit in, following the When-In-Rome Principle. In particular, you should take a stab at the accent.

Unless, of course, your travels don't require you to change languages. We expect students learning German and Chinese to pronounce things like Berliners and Beijingians, but for some reason, when Americans hoof it to Great Britain, taking on their local accent is *verboten*. All it does is turn you into what we call a pompous ass (or, more locally, *arse*). Strangely, the reverse does not hold, and Brits coming to the US are allowed to dilute their accent over time, maybe even adopting ours. That's normal enough, I guess. After all, they're finally letting down their hair, no longer forced to pretend they belong to the prop department of the BBC.

The accent police may be on patrol everywhere, but their headquarters are definitely in Paris, and they even threaten natives with their billy club of elocution. A friend of mine hails from Narbonne, down near the border with Spain—a place where R's come with a Spanish trill and vowels hum in the nose. But Thomas speaks like your typical

buttoned-down Parisian, only his grin and affability betray-
ing his origins. "I lost it," he said of his native patter, "when I
came to Paris." He didn't mean that it went missing, the way
you lose an umbrella; no, he ditched it, the way a criminal
tosses evidence into the river before agents from the *Eff-Bee-
Eye* close in.

The problem is going to get worse before it gets—well,
let's be honest, it's never going to get better. Languages have
always snuck over borders, engaging in eyebrow-raising mis-
cegenation, so you may as well get used to it. These days,
thanks to the internet and telecommunications and low-
cost airlines and pretty much everything else, all bets are

off. Hordes of words scuttle across those dashed lines on the map, and no wall is going to stop them. It's a fait accompli. At dinner parties you get button-holed by a guy in *le marketing*, and he yacks about some *nouvelle startup*—one with an exciting *business plan*. It has become de rigueur to discuss *les piercings* of your host's teenage daughter, which make her look like a femme fatale, or *le coming-out* of your co-worker's son. Worse, *les reality shows* on *télévision* have delivered the coup de grâce to high culture, not to mention haute couture and even haute cuisine. Everywhere you look, the hive has been moved six inches or more, and you realize, finally, that this is what's been killing the bees! And, in the bargain, you.

In such conversations I attempt to ping-pong between languages and accents, but I don't have the savoir-faire, or else the savoir-vivre, that it requires. I'm missing a little...I don't know...a little...je ne sais quoi. Yes, that's it. So my pronunciation ends up halfway between Paree and New Joyzee, and as the wrong sounds tumble from my *bouche*, I feel like a *bûche*, or even a bit like George Bush. And that, I can assure you, is no *happy end*.

Squirrel Pie and
the Golden Derrière

AT THE CHEESE SHOP THE OTHER DAY, a woman with a strong chin and dark curls labored over my order. First she cut a strip of potent *Comté* with a double-handled scimitar better suited to removing a king's head. Next came the crumbly *Roquefort*, which she sliced with a wire garrote. (All her tools seemed designed for more sinister purposes.) When she turned and asked me what else I'd like, I reviewed the landscape of wheels and pyramids.

My gaze fell upon something new—a stippled little hockey puck of beige.

"*Qu'est-ce que c'est?*" I asked.

When her eyes lit up, I realized my blunder. Alas, too late.

"Well," she said, sucking in a breath. "For starters, it's cow's milk." That was the last thing I fully understood before the hail of information. It was a "pressed" cheese, she explained, rather than a "cooked" one, produced deep in the Alps, beyond Grenoble, near the Chartreuse monastery, where the liqueur used to be distilled. She took another gulp of air and plunged back in, telling me how much fat the cheese had, in what conditions it had been aged, how the molds formed on the crust, which way the mountainside faced, how much the cows ate for breakfast, and what their names were.

"I'll take one," I said, hoping to close the breach before the tide of details reached my chin.

"In France," she went on, her dimples deepening with excitement, "we eat it with a bit of jam"—and then she was suggesting flavors, launching into the technology of fruit preservation.

"Okay," I said. "Two."

"In France," she harped, "you can make a whole meal out of it."

It was time for the ejection button. I patted my pocket in mock surprise and pulled out my phone, pressing it to my ear. "What?" Then I forced my eyebrows up and spaced out my words. "Oh...my...God! I'll be right there." I looked at the cheese lady and pointed accusingly at the phone, giving the universal gesture for "It's not my fault." Her shoulders rounded, but she conceded to ring me up.

I'm not proud of lies like this, but sometimes that's the price of self-preservation.

As a kid, whenever I told my dad more than he wanted to hear, he'd cut me off. "Just tell me the time," he'd say. "Not how to build a watch." Sometimes I like to imagine how Dad would have fared stranded in France, where they don't merely tell you how to build that watch, but also how to design it, how to smelt the metal for the cogs, and how to make that ticky noise, all before wrapping up with an explanation of how minutes are tied to the rotation of the planet.

You could kind of understand this if the person you're talking to happens to be a watchmaker, but here it's just as likely to be an Uber driver or a mailwoman. People take pleasure in teaching you about things, and if you're a foreigner, their eyes close happily as they open each sentence with, "*In France...*" Should the conversation turn to certain national subjects (cheese, for instance—or wine, sausage, colonialism, World War II, steel-hulled ships, or atomic energy), you want to stand back so you don't get splashed by their enthusiasm.

Back when we bought our apartment, our friends Guy and Sabine came over with a housewarming gift. Hoping for a bottle of wine, I hid my disappointment when Guy grinned impishly and whipped out, of all things, a book. (Quaintly enough, people still read in France.) The volume was all about the area we now lived in, and it told how a river known as the Bièvre used to cut through this neighborhood en route to the Seine. That's why there'd been tanneries close by, not to mention windmills on the hill, quail in the woods, yadda yadda yadda. At least, I assume that's what it said. Guy was reeling off all the information, shoveling details into me as if he'd already read the damn book—or possibly even written it.

It's all part of the pedagogic reflex, which in France is as common as acid reflux, an involuntary burping up of knowledge. In this part of the world people are still infatuated with knowing things, whereas in the States we have outsourced that pesky task to Google.

It's René Descartes' fault. When he came along, back in, oh, whenever it was (if you really want to know, ask a French person), he laid a foundation for figuring everything out, conquering your problems step by goddamned step. Pretty soon you could be absolutely sure about absolutely everything. Knowing stuff became important. Even today it's a linchpin of French identity: I know, therefore I am.

I'm not just referring to know-it-alls, which also exist here, under the names Monsieur or Madame "Je-Sais-Tout."

They are as much a blight in France as elsewhere on the planet. But in France, even ordinary people accumulate bits of knowledge the way they might collect stamps, pasting in their trophies one tiny square at a time. No one has them all, of course, but certain knowledge stamps are more or less required for being French, and each person then develops his own niche—the way people's stamp albums branch into Chilean airmail or South African shipping labels. And as any collector knows, half the fun is sharing your triumphs with others. It's what we call education.

French schools don't just promote the passion for information collection, they provide you with your own starter kit. That's because kids here still memorize things, including whole poems they recite for class, lists of kings, and the dates of big events. We witnessed this first-hand as our daughter underwent brainwashing in the cult of knowledge during the eighth grade. Over dinner she would lecture us about the universal rights of citizens, or the history of silt deposits on the Nile, or even...well, God only knows. We weren't really paying attention.

In any case, that's a far cry from the US, where memorization is so routinely pooh-poohed that many of us barely remember attending school at all. During my own early education, only a couple of facts stuck, and it wasn't information likely to help me get ahead. The first cropped up in a fourth-grade report about Davy Crockett, which I plagiarized from the *World Book Encyclopedia* with the precision of a medieval scribe. Even now I recall how the words traveled straight from my eyes to the tip of my number 2 pencil. Then I paused over the words I'd copied, my eyes widening. Crockett, the august authorities asserted, had grown up so poor that his impoverished family sometimes ate *squirrel pie*. My imagination bubbled over. At last, a detail worth remembering! This delicacy became the focus of my report, and when I brought home a B for my work, Mom offered to make a celebratory dish, and I requested the obvious. (To her credit, it wasn't even the squirrels that threw her off. *We don't have pie for dinner*, she shot back.)

The second notable *oeuvre* from my elementary days was a one-act play I wrote about the rollicking adventures of Sir Francis Drake. The only historically accurate detail was the ship's name, the *Golden Hind*, which allowed me to declaim what I took to be a synonym for *butt* in front of the entire class, generating the kind of tittering usually reserved for the word titter. Boy, Sir Francis sure loved talking about that ship!

I graduated from elementary school with decent grades. Nobody cared about facts, so I fit right in.

So, while little French kids were busy pasting hard-earned stamps onto the pages of their knowledge album, in the US we just made things up. It's like that poster that hung in my school's media center, the one that said, "Knowledge is the accumulation of facts, but wisdom is knowing how to find them." This was an influential quote in my childhood, although I can't recall who said it. It pretty much exonerated me from knowing anything, urging me to take the wisdom route, which had the added benefit of sounding like the high road. Like me, lots of Americans get huffy about folks who know too much and who make sure you know they know it. Short and sweet, that's the American motto. Politicians have learned this especially well. Some of them are naturally stupid of course, but others go out of their way to dumb things down for fear of being branded a wonk or an elitist or, worst of all, a Francophile.

One of the most annoying things about French knowledge is how much of it is tied to history. It's not enough to collect your stamps—you have to arrange them in chronological order and even know something about their production. Because I try to be a good friend, I cracked open that book Guy had given me about our neighborhood. It was a kind of coffee-table volume—you could tell because it included pictures, which is a concession French publishers make only when they're aiming for a lowbrow readership. (A famous travel guide series, the *Guide du Routard*, includes no photographs at all in order to leave more room for facts.) But even so, Guy's book got technical fast, starting in 1376 and then presenting six hundred years' worth of maps, statistics, and public works, explaining how the city diverted or covered over this old waterway in our neighborhood, erasing it entirely from view. There'd been some urban planning, and somehow it was all connected to the construction of sewers. Water still flowed toward the Seine, but entirely underground. The bottom line was that, before looking at this book, I had no idea there was a river here, and afterwards I understood that there wasn't. The Bièvre drained away invisibly—just like all the details that slipped through the fishnet of my memory. It was hard to imagine trotting this information out at cocktail parties.

I retired the book to my shelf. I hadn't retained many of the facts, but at least I'd know where to find them—which, after all, was the definition of wisdom.

For an American I'm pretty tolerant of knowledge, but even I have a hard time with certain situations. Guided tours in France are the worst. Sometimes I get stuck accompanying visitors for a bus tour of the city—or worse, a Bateau Mouche. Some information specialist drones on over the loudspeaker, and my eyes glaze over. For the eight-hundredth time I'll hear how tall the Eiffel Tower is or how many tons of iron it took to build it, and five minutes later my brain will snap back to its virginal state, entirely untainted. Sometimes even my American visitors are surprised. "When did she say this was built?" they'll whisper to me thirty seconds after the guide has told them. When I confess I have no idea, they are slightly affronted. It's OK for facts to slip from *their* brain like an egg from a non-stick pan, but I'm supposed to know better because I'm sort of a local.

The American disregard for detail raises some eyebrows here. To the French mind, facts are bricks in the rampart of knowledge, each one crucial to the integrity of the structure. It's not enough to be an expert about Davy Crockett's tarte à la squirrel and Sir Francis Drake's Golden Derrière—you're also expected to know something about…well, whatever else it was that got Crockett and Drake into the record books.

However, Americans are not total idiots. We're merely interested in something other than details. Americans like to *get the feel* of things. That's why living museums are so popular in the States. Why waste a bunch of time reading books about Benjamin Franklin when you could just go and yack with him in person? To the American way of thinking, French education is like one of those pointillist paintings by Seurat—an oddly precise yet bloodless picture composed of a million dots. Americans prefer Monet—those vague and watery images where everything runs together but still gives you the gist of things. Americans want the Big Picture, even if it's a bit blurry.

A Parisian I know was asked to give a talk to a group of American students. Philippe is a specialist on Jews in France, and because he wanted to make sure the encounter went well, he asked me for advice. Though he's a large fellow with the kind of beard that announces confidence, his eyes showed terror.

"I know American students are different," he said. "What am I supposed to do?"

"Don't slather on the facts," I warned him. "Americans like things to be interactive. They want to participate."

The answer rattled him. "Interactive?" he mumbled to himself as he moved to the front of the room. Students were already filing in. "*Participate?*"

I pulled up a chair. They didn't really need me for this class, but I wasn't going to miss it for anything.

He began with a little lecture about the history of Jews in France. Philippe had done this talk a million times for French students, and he had it down pat—all the dates and famous people. Soon he was revved up, reaching cruising speed for information delivery. There was so much to cover in the next half hour! But after a few minutes the students were fidgeting in their seats. One young woman snuck her cell phone from her backpack and was scrolling through Facebook. Philippe sensed he was losing them and he started to panic, which meant going faster and faster, as though the trick to capturing their attention was to give them more and more, cramming it in as if they were geese whose livers he needed to fatten. *Too many dots*, I wanted to cry out. *Less Seurat, more Monet!* I caught his eye and made a scissors with my fingers. He paused, stricken, and then started again with hesitation. I saw him swallow hard as he began eliminating things. Specific dates were the first to go. Maybe it was enough for students to know in what decade the Dreyfus Affair started. Or maybe just what century. He swallowed down the names of some of the second-tier political figures. The students were a little more attentive now, though it was hard to say what had caught their eye. Was it the information he'd been scattering like handfuls of grain? Or was it the wincing look on his face? Each time he sacrificed a fact, he grimaced as if he'd lopped off one of his own fingers.

When he finished, the room was perfectly still, and Philippe's eyes darted back and forth, wondering from what side the students might attack. Because he'd cut so much out, there were ten minutes left. I could tell the cogs were spinning as he pondered his next move. From the back of the room I drew a question mark in the air. He went ashen, as though I'd pronounced a death sentence.

"Any…"—his voice cracked, and he looked like he was in the midst of a painful bowel movement—"…questions?"

For a while the only sound was the fluorescent light buzzing overhead.

Finally a student's hand went up. She wanted to know about Philippe's background, how he got into this work.

The question stymied him. That wasn't the topic on the table. The talk wasn't about *him*, it was about *history*. But he stammered out a sentence or two, and the girl nodded.

Another student had a question, more on topic. This time Philippe answered with a five-hundred-word essay, complete with footnotes. A third question produced a second essay, somewhat longer. He was back in his element, the captain of his own Golden Hind. But that put an end to it—no one was foolish enough to raise a hand a fourth time.

As they left, he staggered back toward me, panting.

"How did it go?" he asked.

"Not bad." And I meant it. He was trying to meet them halfway.

"Any thoughts about how could I make it more…"—he cringed—"…interactive?"

I stroked my chin. "I suppose you could try asking *them* a question. Sort of like a conversation."

By the way his beard sank, I could tell this went too far. Why on earth would he ask *them* anything? Hadn't they come to hear *him*? He was the scholar, the specialist. They were the empty vessels he was meant to fill.

"It's like Davy Crockett," I explained. "You can only reach Americans at their own level."

He searched my eyes with his. "What do you mean?"

I put it as plainly as I could. "You have to start with the squirrels."

For an American, it's not at all clear how to thread the cultural needle. I'm reminded of a friend who came to Paris and put her daughters in the local schools. After the first day, the older one came home shell-shocked, lamenting how much French she was going to have to learn. The younger one, infinitely more practical, showed up with a look of grim satisfaction. "How did it go?" her mother asked. "Well, it's going to be a lot of work," she said, putting her fists on her hips, "but by the end of the year, I'll have taught them all English."

That's the question: Do we become them, or should they become us? The two systems are like joining a metric bolt with an American nut. They look like they ought to fit, but after the first couple of turns, they bind up.

I tell people the systems are equally good, but that's not how I feel in the midst of humiliations. Usually it happens at a dinner party somewhere. The guests are debating the merits of various Merovingian kings or the articles of the European Constitution. Eager to join the fray, I make the mistake of raising my finger to ask for some kind of clarification. In the States there's no such thing as a stupid question, but that's not the case in France. Usually the question I ask makes the table go still, and people stare down at their plates out of embarrassment, as if I'd just released a gust of intestinal exhaust.

In my fantasies it's everybody else who gusts. There will be an obscure conversation about Charles de Gaulle, and I'll intervene with, "Yes, and wasn't his dog named Pepper?" Their mouths will round with amazement. "This cheese," I'll tell the lady at the shop, "it tastes like it came from the south wall of the aging cave." She starts asking me for recommendations. Sometimes the fantasies soar to even giddier heights. In these, I don't just place a cherry on top of the cake of knowledge; I actually knock someone else's cherry off. It should happen quite publicly—preferably in a lecture hall or on television. Some blowhard will be prattling on, making rising circles with his hand, and I'll lean forward. "Excuse me," I'll say, "I believe you meant to refer to the troglodytic drawings in the grotto of Lascaux," and he will blanch.

But for this to happen, I'd actually have to add some stamps to my collection. I would need to know a few things—or at least be better at Googling them really fast on my phone. Instead, I've gone a different route: I make things up.

Not long ago we had dinner with friends, and while Anne helped Pascale get the coffee going, Jacques was talking to me about the history of Paris. While he expounded about architecture and urban planning, I uttered the occasional "uh-huh" or "you don't say," the way a circus performer gives the occasional touch to a spinning plate.

He pointed out their living room window at the Rue de Vaugirard, which he claimed was the longest street in Paris, cutting from the edge of town and going right toward the center.

"Do you know *why?*" he quizzed me with a sly grin.

Why *what*? I mulled over possible answers. Because all cities have roads? Because lots of them probably go toward the center? Because one of them has to be the longest?

The dinner they'd given me had been delicious, so I decided I should reciprocate with a small gift of my own. "No," I sighed. "Tell me."

And he did. It had to do with pilgrimages to Notre-Dame Cathedral, ages ago. People would stream in from the plains, throngs of them trudging toward that steeple on the Seine.

A bubble of memory wiggled its way to the surface of my brain. It had to do with that book Guy had given me all those months ago—the one about roads and rivers in our neighborhood. I kind of remembered it, but the details were vague, like a Monet painting. I did have wisdom on my side, for I knew where the facts were located; unfortunately, they sat on a bookshelf halfway across the city. For now, I was going to have to wing it, adding dots of knowledge on my own.

"Speaking of roads," I began. Then I listed a few streets in my own neighborhood that formed a straightish line to the Seine—though not toward Notre-Dame. "Any idea why they're aligned?"

Jacques' eyes gleamed.

With great care I unfolded my explanation of the Bièvre, of this river that had fueled the tanneries and mills, and that had disappeared more than a century ago, paved over by streets that led toward the Seine.

He nodded hungrily. Not wanting to disappoint, I told him more and more, squeezing out new facts from the few details I kind of remembered. I could practically see his stalactite of knowledge growing.

Best of all, when I got back home and pulled out the book, I found I'd been about 25% right—a lot better than I'd done in my play about Sir Francis Drake's backside.

I wondered what my dad would have thought. It turns out that if you go into enough detail about how the watch is made, nobody checks to see if it works. They don't even care what time it is.

Living here has taught me to become specifically vague, foggily precise—combining the best of France and America.

Or is it the worst? Frankly, it's hard to tell.

Some Assembly Required

IT STARTED WITH MERDE—buckets of it. Dave had borrowed our place while we were on vacation, and he called in a panic. Sewage was backing up, and he was bailing.

"How's that even possible?" I said. After all, the apartment was on the third floor. Had I missed a news flash about the City of Light foundering in a sea of filth? What had become of those giant sewers, the ones so big that Jean Valjean could run through them in *Les Misérables*?

Turned out the building had a gastric problem, and an old drainpipe proved to be the weak link. Dave contained the tsunami with a plastic plug and a roll of duct tape, known locally as *scotch américain*.

When we returned, I crept to the end of the hallway and creaked open the door. A bulge showed where the tape bound the pipe. It was holding—for the moment.

I hadn't thought about this room for months—not since we'd added on the tiny apartment next door to gain a bedroom for our daughter. But since we didn't need two kitchens, I'd stripped out the cabinets and countertops before abandoning it. Now it looked like one of those bombed-out ruins you see on the History Channel—gutted, the ceiling sick with leprosy, tiles lifting from the walls, the plaster wounded, wires dangling where appliances used to live, varicose veins of copper pipe running along the baseboard. A behemoth basin of chipped ceramic sat enthroned in one corner, cemented in place back when the building went up.

"Come to think of it," Anne said, "we could turn this into a guest bedroom."

By "we" she meant "you," and by "you" I mean "me."

Worst of all, she was right. So, the next day I cracked my knuckles and the project began: the former kitchen would wrap itself in a chrysalis of plastic sheeting, later to emerge as a butterfly, or at least a moth.

Like my wife, I often wish I were my brother-in-law. He enters projects like a gunslinger, palms poised over the sides of a hip-hugging tool belt. Back in the States, he owns a four-by-four truck, useful for schlepping ladders and generators and air compressors, all of which he owns, probably in duplicate. In Paris, my workshop consists of a drawer in the kitchen. It's jammed with (as I look in it now) picture hooks, wire, Ikea hinges, old screwdrivers, a putty knife, a broken pair of pliers, and a hammer. Somewhere else (I can never remember where) a hacksaw and a few other tools have made a nest for themselves. In addition to being inexperienced at home repair, I am ill-equipped.

I am also stingy, which makes for a troubling combination. In Paris, if you have enough money, you can find people to do just about anything. When we expanded our quarters, for instance, we paid a company to create a passageway between the two apartments, opening the wall that supported the six stories above us. But the bill left me clutching my chest from angina. This new job I'd have to do myself.

Home projects in France fall under the general category of *bricolage*. The word comes from a medieval term for a catapult, which makes you feel important and battle-worthy. When Guy and Sabine invited us to a movie that night, I declined heroically, announcing: "*Je fais du bricolage.*"

"You?" Sabine snorted. "This I have to see."

My French friends think I'm even more incompetent than I really am, and it's partly because of vocabulary. I manage pretty well in the local tongue, but everyday objects can still leave me staring like a mute. And when I don't know the word for, say, a Phillips-head screwdriver, people leap to the conclusion that I've never before seen such a contraption. (Turns out it's called a *tournevis cruciforme*, a term that, in my addled brain, conjures up centurions fastening Jesus to the cross with screws. After all, they do hold better than nails.)

My secret weapon is named Jérôme. He wears a yellow vest and works at the *Bricorama*, the hardware store closest to me, a direct competitor for the *Monsieur Bricolage* chain, and for *Brico Dépôt*, or my favorite, *Leroy Merlin*, which translates as The King-Merlin, evoking Arthurian legend. A man's home really is his castle, and castles need upkeep.

I say "hardware store," but like all translations this one is approximate. Paris doesn't believe in actual hardware stores, the ones where you shuffle through in your grease-smeared clothes with paint in your hair while searching for a cotter pin. In the States, nails and screws are often heaped in bins, and you rake them up with a claw, buying what you need by weight. Or else you pick your nits, going up to the cash register with two nails of different sizes, a lock-washer, a carriage bolt, and maybe a single chrome-plated, reverse-threaded, metric hex-nut. Somehow, they have everything: You can spend an hour poring through plastic bins of widgets and doohickeys, plucking out just the ones you need to build your thingamajig.

At the *Bricorama* all the hardware is sealed in plastic. The first time I straggled in, seeking to replace a single mangled bolt, Jérôme arched his eyebrow in disbelief, as though I'd asked to borrow the Mona Lisa for the weekend. He proposed a package of twelve bolts that looked similar but different. Because they were vacuum-sealed, I couldn't do a side-by-side comparison. Were they the same? Jérôme's eyes narrowed as he held up the package to the light. "It's hard to say," he concluded with a shrug. And he was right.

Jérôme is not a specialist, but he knows a little about everything. For the transformation of the ancient kitchen, he packed me like a mule crossing the Andes: plaster repair mix, tubs of skim-coat, an application knife, hacksaw blades, outlet covers, primer, buckets of paint—not to mention plugs, stoppers and resins to handle the plumbing issue that had started it all.

I got to work. The first job was to remove the ceramic basin—half kitchen sink, half laundry tub, including a yard-long stretch where dishes could dry or where you might pound dirty loincloths with a rock. The thing was anchored to the walls, and the more I chiseled toward the metal struts connecting it to the building, the less sure I was I wouldn't pop through into the neighbor's kitchen on the other side.

You have to be careful about things like that. Apartment buildings are divided between the *parties communes*—all the shared stuff like elevators and stairways and internal plumbing—and the *parties privatives*—the "private parts" that belong to your unit, and that you protect as fiercely as your genitals. The difference sounds clear enough: the *parties communes* are on the outside, the *parties privatives* closer to home. Sometimes it's simple: when the woman on the fifth floor (known in hissed conversations as *la dame du cinquième*) established a beachhead in the *parties communes* by keeping a dresser in the hallway, she committed an obvious border infraction. Other cases are more ambiguous. For instance, a pipe running right through my bathroom doesn't actually belong to me: it's a *partie commune*. And a chunk of our property is a stall in the basement four floors below. In this way an apartment building resembles the EU, where smidgens of Europe end up in the West Indies, or big chunks in the middle (like Switzerland) don't belong at all.

Our building association has rules, one of which restricts *bricolage* to day-time hours and forbids it on Sundays, which means you're free to engage in *bricolage* at any time except for when you might actually have time to engage in it. This was a problem for removing the sink, which required the kind of drilling, hammering, and sawing that couldn't be masked by loud coughs or the roar of the hair dryer. I synchronized my hammering with the church bells, which meant that every hour I could get off four, five, or six good whacks, depending.

The sink wasn't budging, so I went back to see Jérôme. He considered my problem, fingertips tented, and then sold me a crowbar and a carbide-tipped drill bit. I excavated the rods of iron during the day, but in the evening I engaged in quieter activities, dislodging tiles from the walls, finding corrugated ribs of cement underneath. The square tiles came off mostly in triangles, breaking in half as I levered them, the remaining half then breaking into smaller triangles as I worked, the triangles growing smaller and smaller like a problem from tenth-grade geometry. By the end I was ankle deep in razor-edged shards of ceramic.

Then came the question of disposal. Getting rid of things in Paris is either simple or impossible, depending. The trash is picked up every evening in our neighborhood, and I sometimes help Monsieur Carvalho, our concierge, roll out the bins. Of course, some things don't fit into the trash cans. These are known as "cumbersome objects," and to rid yourself of them you have to contact the city in advance, place the item on the sidewalk, and tape a registration number to it. The service is entirely free, presumably to keep people from tossing old washing machines into the Seine the way they used to. Back in the States I pay two bucks every time I put out an extra lunch bag of garbage, but in Paris you could leave a dead elephant on the sidewalk as long as you stick a number on it, and two guys in coveralls will whiz by to cart it away on a flatbed truck.

Except, that is, for rubble. Building materials will not be taken by anyone, and you're supposed to haul the stuff to the dump yourself. The task is technically possible even if, like me, you don't own a car: I could, hypothetically, lug a fifty-pound sack ten minutes to the Metro station, take a ride to the edge of town, tote it up the steps, walk a kilometer, and arrive at the dump located under an elevated portion of the ring road. In this way, not counting stops at the pharmacy and the chiropractor, you might dispose of a kitchen's worth of tile and plaster over the course of two or three days. Instead, I drew my inspiration from *The Great Escape*, the way the prisoners tunneled out of the stalag, disposing of dirt by trickling it down their pant legs as they strolled about the grounds. The notion of those razor-shards tumbling down my trousers sent a tingle through my *parties privatives*, but the general idea was good, so over the course of a few days I slipped extra sacks into the garbage bins downstairs. On those days I volunteered to help Monsieur Carvalho even more energetically. "*Non, non!*" I'd cry, flapping him away. "Let *me* take that one."

One day Guy and Sabine came by when I was halfway through the project, and Guy helped me tug the ceramic sink to the elevator. We dragged it like a cadaver. Out on the curb I taped a "cumbersome object" number to it. When we returned upstairs, Sabine was at the doorway to the room, shaking her head. It's true the place looked worse now. The doors from the larder under the window were gone, and the walls were straight out of Aleppo. Flakes of plaster from the ceiling had gathered on the floor like pale autumn leaves. This was the dark-night-of-the-soul moment, that torturous period of self-doubt. But what could I do? Restore the sink? Glue back the bits of tile in a crazy mosaic? No, no. Unless I was willing to seal it up like a Pharaoh's tomb, I had to push ahead.

"Tell me again what you're putting here?" Sabine said.

I proclaimed it would be a bedroom for guests.

She snorted again. "Do you have friends who like to sleep standing up?"

The quip seemed uncalled for, but then I measured, and Sabine was right. I'd imagined turning this former kitchenette into a cozy hideaway, but it was looking Anne-Frankish in its dimensions. Grains of reality caught in the cogs of my imagination. It would be desirable, for example, that the bedroom door should be closeable, but how that might occur once a bed was in place strained the imagination. Another nice feature would include accessing the window without crawling over the mattress. Equally unlikely. I experimented with ideas for Murphy beds and Japanese contraptions that floated down from the ceiling.

Finding a bed that might fit turned into a fairy-tale quest. The corners of the room made the job especially problematic: doors and radiators got in the way, and in the corner where the sink had been (and where the sewage had gushed), water pipes jutted out.

In the States it's hard to fathom the millimetric precision of Paris decorating. Americans are used to living rooms where they need a cell phone to call their kids slouching on the other end of the sectional. But in Paris the ideal decorator would be a former U-Boat engineer—someone used to outfitting cramped quarters. Every cranny counts, and Parisians quibble so fiercely over smidgens of space that whenever an apartment is sold, a professional geometer is called in to reckon the surface area of the oddly shaped rooms. Money is a big part of it: a square centimeter of real estate can cost close to two euros in the better parts of Paris (i.e., not where I live), which sounds like a bargain till you do the math and realize there are 10,000 centimeters to a meter. A square yard of Paris costs as much as a well-equipped Peugeot. If you buy an older apartment that has weathered many generations of occupants, you can sometimes increase its value just by scraping off thick layers of wallpaper.

In my case, I needed half a centimeter if a bed was going to fit. At the *Bricorama* Jérôme proposed various products to remove the ribs of adhesive left by the tiles, which would gain me a touch more room. The stuff had somehow fossilized, so I took to chipping it off, doing so with the care of a sculptor finishing the buttocks of the Venus de Milo. Unfortunately, the Venus's cheeks were developing a serious case of acne. To smooth it out in the end, I unsheathed the mudding knife, and with the great swooshing gestures of a man wielding a saber, I smeared on joint compound.

Old kitchens are veined with electrical lines, and though I know nothing about electricity, it doesn't bother me to brandish wire cutters over a collection of cables, pausing like Tom Cruise as he defuses a bomb. I snipped happily, and pretty much at random. It's true that electrical work can be dangerous, but at least if you make a serious mistake, you don't have to live with it—especially in France where the voltage is jacked up to thin the population.

The thing I'd avoided so far was the plumbing, which is my most hated form of *bricolage*.

There were water pipes everywhere. Some ran along the ceiling before angling down to where the washing machine and dishwasher used to be. One went through a wall to the WC. Another entered the plaster mysteriously, never to re-emerge. And some had been decommissioned, back when the water service was updated.

Because the room was no longer a kitchen, I didn't need a skein of plumbing. I contacted the building management company to find out which pipes were *parties communes* and which were *privatives*. And especially, which ones were still active. Their email response was cryptic, advising me that I could remove the lines that were "no longer in use," but declining to identify them. They added a perky little warning: "Be sure you don't cut the wrong ones!"—punctuated with a smiley face.

I sawed off pipes and sealed them with fittings provided by Jérôme, concealing the stubs behind layers of plaster.

Like a mass murderer, I hoped that burying these body parts would be the end of it. And mostly it was. Even the waste line that had started it all disappeared behind a coating of white.

Only one problem remained. On the pipe coming from the water meter, someone had installed a bulky saddle valve sticking out precisely where the bed had to go. Removing the valve would resolve the final space problem, but at the cost of triggering a permanent geyser.

This one stumped even Jérôme. There was no way out: I needed a professional.

In the States, you retain a plumber the way you book a venue for a wedding—twelve or eighteen months out. But here I went down the street to the bathroom remodeling shop, and they agreed to send around "their man" to take a look. An hour later my phone rang. The plumber wanted me to buzz him up. Moments later, a garden gnome walked in, a hundred years old and shorter than my daughter. "Shall we examine the patient?" he asked, and I led him to it.

Most plumbers I've encountered travel with a treasure chest of tools, but this one held a leather pouch the size of a lunch bag. He opened the flap to reveal two screwdrivers (one was *cruciforme*), a battered pair of pliers, and a tiny mallet. In comparison, my kitchen drawer of tools was an entire *Bricorama*. After turning the water off, he removed the saddle valve and pondered the hole lengthily in a pose reminiscent of Rodin's Thinker.

"I believe I can cut it here," he said, drawing a line with his finger. "And add a piece. When I'm done, it will just stick out a bit more."

But sticking out more was impossible! I couldn't lose any centimeters. The vision of the bed dimmed in my thoughts. Sabine was right. Guests would have to sleep standing up. I stammered a protest.

He caressed his double chin. "All right, all right. Let me try something else…" Out the door he went, soon to reappear with an acetylene torch and a few sticks of metal. He played a blue flame over the pipe. Steam rose, and when the sizzling stopped, an acrid smell filled the air. He moved a rod of copper to the opening and applied the flame, making the metal weep golden droplets around the rim of the hole, then inside the rim of that rim, making the hole smaller and smaller, the O shrinking like a closing mouth, until all that remained was a pucker of gold. He stood.

"There."

"Will it hold?"

He shrugged. "Should."

The pipe still didn't hug the wall, and this inefficiency cost a crucial centimeter right where the bed had to fit. I pointed this out, and the gnome nodded—a man well versed in Parisian battles for space. With leathery hands he gripped the freshly repaired copper—still hot to the touch—and began to wrestle with it, shoving hard until the metal budged. Not satisfied, he drew the mallet from his pouch and began a series of full swings, hammering on it like a blacksmith. With each blow the pipe shrank closer to the wall, bending at the brittle new scab.

"It's not going to break, is it?"

He paused in his pounding and shrugged again. "Shouldn't."

There were finishing touches. A gallon of sludge treated the psoriasis of the walls. Paint went on. The little window sprouted curtains, and a light fixture appeared. I found the one bed in all of France that might fit the space, and after a little customization, it did.

Sabine came by, nodding as she took it in. "Looks like a room on a ship," she said. "In steerage."

She was kind of right.

For its maiden voyage, I slept there myself. After all, if the boat went down, the captain should sink along with it. In the dark of night, with the door closed and the curtains drawn, it felt like a Jules Verne adventure, twenty thousand leagues under the sea. The bed listed a bit to starboard. There were a few clanks in the walls, along with a whoosh whenever the neighbors flushed their toilet. But for now at least, the seams of the Nautilus held.

The Medi-Morphosis

AN ACHE WOKE ME FROM TROUBLED DREAMS, and when I shifted, a bolt of lightning shot past my kidneys into my lower back. On the pain scale, it registered between a volcanic eruption and a supernova. Like an overturned beetle, I wriggled my limbs and moaned.

In the States you might go straight for the cymbal crash of 911, but the French prefer their medicine to crescendo slowly, like Ravel's *Bolero*. So I crawled to the phone and dialed my local GP. His machine answered, and the recording alone served as a balm. Docteur Pédron has the invigorating voice of someone who has schussed his way down a black diamond ski run, and it's hard not to feel peppy in his presence, even recorded.

Since his office wasn't open yet, I relaxed on the floor and pondered my lot. My predicament wasn't altogether surprising. I'd spent the previous two weeks converting the old kitchen into a guest room—a task that transformed me into a pack animal for rubble and building supplies. So, after decades of loyal service, my back had rebelled.

Part of me was tempted to commando-crawl to the airport and return home. After all, the glitz of American medicine wows me like a Broadway show, one where the eye-popping ticket prices promise quality. But it turns out the reviews are only so-so. The US may be first in cost, but the World Health Organization ranks us thirty-seventh for quality—just ahead of archrival Slovenia. It's like paying *Hamilton* prices but only getting bad seats at *King Kong*. In fact, it's the French who get the best show in town. They don't make the podium for cost (a measly fourth place), but for quality they take the gold. And since I was already in that promised land, I decided to try my luck with the socialists.

Docteur Jean-Jacques Pédron is my entry point into the medical system here. For years, I have brought my ills to his office, which is located near the Grand Mosque of Paris—a towering white structure with a first-rate café. Usually, I treat myself to mint tea and almond-paste cookies before medical checkups, but today I skipped the snack and went straight to his door, pressing the button for the bell. A camera allows Pédron to screen new arrivals on the sidewalk, but the latch clicked open before I could even peer into the lens. So much for security.

Frankly, doctor visits in France can seem primitive to Americans. When stateside, I go to a clinic so large that a hostess is stationed by the carpeted entrance. She directs me to the appropriate bank of receptionists, where another young woman swipes my insurance card and my American

Express before presenting me with a clipboard. After serving myself a latte at the beverage station, I settle into an armchair and ponder the questionnaire. *How often do you feel nervous?* it asks. *How often do you feel hopeless?* These probing queries reassure me of the importance of *me*, a crucial topic for Americans, and though I'm never sure which answer is considered correct, I appreciate the opportunity to reflect on them. Eventually, a nurse sings out my name and we travel through various stations, measuring my weight, my height, my pulse, my blood pressure. Then I strip to my underwear and sit alone until the High Priest to whom I report enters. He's robed in a white coat and wears a stethoscope.

At Docteur Pédron's, on the other hand, you step straight from the sidewalk into his waiting room. It's a cramped square space furnished with metal chairs, yellowing wallpaper, framed posters of ski resorts, and a coffee table groaning under back issues of *Elle*, *L'Express*, and *Santé*. In one corner, there stands a plastic houseplant desperate for dusting. Another permanent fixture is the patients, for the waiting room is never empty, even when I arrive at the hour of opening—as though the current occupants were left over from the previous day.

In waiting lounges in the US, I studiously ignore the presence of other people. On the rare occasion a person I know enters the room, I become consumed by the urgency of answering my clipboard questions. In France, however, your arrival is acknowledged by nods or even mumbled greetings, and those already present keep their eye on you. This is to discourage cutting in line, which could technically be possible, for Docteur Pédron has no receptionist to check you in for your appointment—and, in fact, no appointments. Usually it's just drop-in time. The American in me wants order—at least a number to be taken, like at the DMV. But here, turn-taking is maintained by a subtle play of nods and frosty stares, a practice so terrible in its efficiency that I have never witnessed an infraction.

Visits take a while, for Pédron is a one-man-band. He's the only doctor, and there are no nurses. When not busy palpating or scoping, he manages the schedule, buzzes people in, produces bills, deciphers the insurance, and replenishes the supply of pamphlets in the waiting room. If specialized tests are needed, he sends you two blocks away to a lab that draws your blood or zaps an X-ray. Your medical information travels in the chip of your *carte vitale*, or Life Card, and the rest gets emailed via the most secure medical messaging system in the world. Healthcare in France is half MacGyver and half NASA.

An hour or so later, it was my turn. The doctor waved for me to follow him. Docteur Pédron is small and fit in a slender, middle-aged sort of way, and he is usually attired in a snappy gray suit, which makes me fear I've pulled him away from a dinner party, or perhaps a funeral.

In his office, I winced myself onto a chair, balancing my vertebrae like a stack of teacups. Settled behind his walnut desk, he lifted his palms in wonder and asked his favorite question: "What on earth are you doing here, Monsieur Carpenter?"

I should mention that Docteur Pédron is perpetually astonished to see me. For him I am a potential cover model for the *Santé* magazines littering the waiting room, rather than a pear-shaped guy strapped into a suicide vest of bad habits. He flaps away descriptions of symptoms like pesky motes of dust. *No, no,* the suave backs of his fingers say, *none of that matters.* Everything I tell him is both boggling and trivial—indeed boggling *because* so trivial.

I began my tale, describing how I woke to find myself transformed into an invertebrate. Meanwhile, Pédron looked up my file. He used to keep the history of my visits on small lined cards, but about ten years ago, he converted everything to computer. Because he types only with his index fingers, I had plenty of time to look about.

American examination rooms try hard to impress. In the clinic I sometimes visit in the States, each room houses an altar for the human body—a table-height bed placed atop a movable block of steel. The walls are pocked with electrical outlets and brackets. The only decoration consists of two anatomical drawings of the human body—provided, I presume, in case the doctor needs reminders during the visit. There are also banks of cupboards under the counter. Although my impromptu inspections have revealed most of these cabinets to be empty, their presence contributes to the general impression of seriousness.

I love Docteur Pédron, but his office is worrisome for its lack of medical paraphernalia. The parquet floor is covered by a tattered Persian rug, and most of the furnishings appear to have been collected from various garage sales: springy daybed, metal coatrack, knickknack cabinet, mismatched dresser. Most of his equipment—stethoscope, depressors, blood pressure gauge—are hidden in desk drawers. And while his bookshelf does include a few medical tomes, these rub shoulders with a volume about home repair, and even several novels.

It's not as if French doctors are stuck in the leeches-and-bleeding era of medicine. Hardly. Not far from Pédron's place of business, you can see the dome of La Salpétrière, the hospital where world-class experts snip tumors from brains, blast growths with ray guns, and splice the occasional gene. Just because it's socialized doesn't mean they don't have the heavy artillery you need when the going gets rough.

General practice offices, however, tend to be a little more homespun. One day, for example, I stopped by because of a pressure in my chest. After asking what on earth I was doing there, Docteur Pédron listened stone-faced to my litany of symptoms. Finally, he sighed and offered to do an EKG. Scenes of self-importance flowered in my imagination: Monsieur Carpenter being wheeled on a gurney to the EKG chamber, Monsieur Carpenter studied by a huddle of experts with clipboards, Monsieur Carpenter immortalized in medical textbooks for self-diagnosis of a rare disease.

But the machine was just a plastic box the size of an alarm clock, stuffed in a drawer of his desk. A few suction cups later, it produced a curl of paper showing peaks and valleys as regular as the Alps. The device looked homemade to my unpracticed eye (was it possible it dispensed pre-printed rolls of regular heartbeat?), but before I could inspect it, he'd tucked everything away and declared me to be in working order. Once again, I was the man crying wolf.

It is inconceivable to Docteur Pédron that any of my complaints should be taken seriously, and because his incredulity is contagious, I always leave his office satisfied. Visits make me feel good about myself. They're like getting a haircut or buying a new pair of tennis shoes—except a good bit cheaper. A standard doctor visit currently costs twenty-five euros in France (one euro after insurance), and the price is the same for house calls, which are still a thing here.

Today, I waited for Pédron to mock my complaints so my back could stop hurting. But as I rattled off the details of my story, the doctor leaned forward, his eyebrows sinking below the rims of his glasses. Where was that dismissive sweep of the hand, the roll of the eyes, the astonished protestations about my excellent health? I downplayed my symptoms and up-played my overreactions, laying the groundwork for him to chuckle it all away.

"Well," he said sternly after my tale. "This time you've done it."

I started unbuttoning my shirt, but he shook his head. I was aghast. Docteur Pédron had never turned down an opportunity to reduce me to a specimen in underwear.

"There is no need," he said.

I protested. Surely if he examined me, he'd find the bulging Lego piece that needed to be shoved back into place. Shouldn't he at least run some tests? Wasn't there a Ronco CAT-scanner in the desk drawer next to that EKG thing?

But no. He just gave his head a shake to underline the hopelessness of it all. For once Monsieur Carpenter hadn't been exaggerating. Without equipment or test results, without even deigning to touch me, Docteur Pédron produced a diagnosis.

"Your back is *bloqué*."

What I'd described, he said, was absolutely classic.

"Probably I just need to work out more," I replied. It was unlike Docteur Pédron to run out of dismissive comments, so I tried to prime the pump. "Strengthen my core. Sit-ups and the like." And because I couldn't remember the word for this exercise, I placed my hands behind my head like a POW on a death march, and bowed Japanesely from the waist—a little pantomime that shot a bolt of pain from my midsection into my butt. I gritted a grin to demonstrate how salutary it could be.

No, no, Docteur Pédron's wagging finger insisted. I wasn't going to exercise my way out of this one. As he launched into a lecture about spines and nerves, a more terrifying

montage of my future blossomed: Monsieur Carpenter lying before a surgeon with a meat cleaver, Monsieur Carpenter unable to wiggle his toes, Monsieur Carpenter wheeled on stage as the poster boy for the telethon. In short, Monsieur Carpenter as the overturned insect, his metamorphosis complete and irreversible.

In fact, Docteur Pédron had something even worse in store. He scribbled on a pad, tore off a sheet, and slid it across the desk. He was sending me to the pharmacy.

If you're into the self-administration of drugs as much as I am, you should never set foot outside the US. It's true we can't tank up on Sudafed the way we used to before the meth-cooking fad took off, but otherwise Americans have a pretty sweet deal. The aisles of a Walgreens or a CVS are like a stroll through a pick-your-own-vegetables farm. You harvest what you want, choosing from among fifty different cough syrups or painkillers. Nearby there's a cornucopia of wart removers and hemorrhoid creams, not to mention antacids, anti-inflammatories, antihistamines, anti-emetics, anti-diarrheals, and, who knows, probably even the Antichrist himself just a little farther down the aisle.

Best of all, unless you're stuck buying prescriptions, you don't have to tell anyone what you're up to. You just stash your hemorrhoid creams and foot fungicides under a box of Froot Loops, and in some places you can even check yourself out via an automated cashier. The secrets of your body are safe.

In France you won't find so much as a roll of Tums at the supermarket, and you can't pop into a 7-Eleven for a little something to snug up your bowels. Pharmacies hold the monopoly on health, and almost everything at the pharmacy lies in the vaults behind the counter. Whenever my body betrays me, I skulk down the street, stand in line, and explain to a lab-coated woman whose bun of hair has been tightened with a wrench exactly what fluids are oozing out of which parts of me. For the benefit of anyone within earshot I provide details about frequency, color, and duration, after which she goes on a scavenger hunt in the back room, returning with a trove of boxes and vials.

Trips to the pharmacy—also government regulated— invariably cost more than trips to the doctor, which perhaps explains why there are even more pharmacies in my neighborhood than there are bakeries (the current score is 18 within a five-minute walk, versus a mere 13 bakeries—and zero full-fledged hardware stores). However, not all of the pharmacies count, because not all of them are real: in France homeopathy is still a thing. That's the eye-of-newt and toe-of-frog style of medicine that French Social Security will still sometimes reimburse, even when it has determined the treatments to be make-believe.

Lucky for me, Docteur Pédron scoffs at homeopathy, so his prescription for my back includes muscle-relaxants and painkillers, along with what he referred to as a belt—not to keep my pants up, but to keep my vertebrae from clattering to the floor. It was in fact a kind of girdle.

I checked my watch. It was almost time for lunch, so I lurched Quasimodo-style down the street to reach the pharmacy before it closed. In France you want to make sure to fall ill during normal working hours—ideally between 9:00 and 1:00, or 3:00 and 7:00, although there are exceptions, so in some neighborhoods the lunch hour doesn't amount to a death sentence.

In line at the pharmacy, my transformation continued. Gravity contracted the remaining portions of my spine, and every movement produced a wince. People around me seemed to be showing off—swaying fluidly to the music of their earbuds, turning their head without rotating their chest, even kneeling to tie their shoes. My own future was devoid of bends or turns. I would slowly petrify. Soon I'd be wearing loafers. My shoulders rounded with despair. When the garments of hope and cheer fall away, all that's left is the homely nakedness of self-pity.

I wanted a nap.

The woman behind the counter had a severe nose but large eyes, making her businesslike in a gentle way, as if she were in charge of financial transactions, but sold only kittens. Her nametag identified her as Béatrice.

"*Vous désirez?*" she said. And although this is a standard shop greeting in France, a way of asking how one can be of service, I was tempted more than ever to sing out that yes, I *did* desire. Vastly. I wished to have my back back. I wanted to feel whole again. I yearned to be able to stand, walk, run, and jump. I longed for college friends and drinking buddies. I wanted to stay out late at jazz clubs. I ached to travel to Italy or Greece on the spur of the moment. I wanted it all.

I slid Docteur Pédron's prescription across the counter. "I would like a girdle," I told her.

She led me down the aisle and pulled out a bin filled with broad bands of fabric, ribbed with elastic and layered with Velcro. There were thick ones and thin ones, narrow and wide. Out came the measuring tape, and soon my attendant was giving me the tailor spin, threading the ribbon of centimeters under my arms and snugging it over my chest, then sliding it to the belly, and finally the hips. She pulled out two or three samples and helped me wriggle into them.

She slipped fingers between the fabric and my flesh to test the constriction, pinching her face when she didn't like the results.

And for once I was glad not to be in an American pharmacy, left to my own devices. Thanks to Béatrice, I ended up with a girdle that fit. True, it was ungainly and plain. It hindered my movements and chafed at my skin. But at the same time, the thing encased my midriff like a protective shell.

In the US, my doctor would likely have prescribed an Iron Man suit, or possibly put me on the waiting list for a full body transplant. And afterward, because of some unfathomable loophole, my insurance would have denied the charges, forcing me to take out a third mortgage or play the lottery. In Paris, though, repairing my body cost about a hundred euros, a sum still leagues beyond what a local would pay, thanks to the national insurance.

The whole thing made me feel strangely un-American. Unbridled capitalism seems great when you're on the winning team. But for those of us who have turned buglike, socialism has a lot to offer.

By the time I walked home from the pharmacy the sun had peeked out, turning the limestone buildings gold. The chill was lifting. The pills had kicked in, and a pleasant grogginess washed over me. Finally, buttressed by the girdle, my torso began to unclench—tentatively at first, but then with trust, and even relief.

All at once it came to me that I was going to survive. Yes, it would take a while. And it might not be easy. But thanks to Docteur Pédron and Béatrice, thanks to my carapace of spandex and straps, I would not be a beetle forever.

The Cartesian Method

I WAS HEADED FOR THE AIRPORT ON THE LIGHT RAIL, and at the last station before a fork in the line a recorded voice announced our destination. It's best to pay attention at this juncture, for if you're on the wrong train, you wind up in the neighboring community of Mitry-Mory—a town so close to the airport that planes screech overhead like diving pterodactyls, but far enough away to make boarding difficult.

After the French recording came the British variant, pronouncing *Charles de Gaulle* as if he were a member of the House of Lords. Then came Italian, the word *treno* followed by an operatic flourish that morphed *Charles de Gaulle* into a member of the mafia. And now, because Paris seeks to be cosmopolitan, the same message trundled along in German, announcing in staccato tones that this train was headed directly for—wait for it—*Marne-la-Vallée/Disneyland*.

A lanky, blue-eyed gentleman leapt to his feet, his face contracted with confusion. The tone had already signaled the closing of the doors, and in a panic, he now bounded

out, his roller bag flying alongside. The doors slid closed, and we departed.

The explanation of this strange pantomime was simple: the unfortunate German traveler had found himself suddenly transported—not to Charles de Gaulle, but to the Twilight Zone.

There is indeed a Disneyland outside of Paris, but it's forty kilometers away in a different direction, not even in the same department. Something had gone wrong in the space-time continuum—as though you were driving to Boston, but thanks to a wormhole on the turnpike you ended up in Hartford.

There was, however, an alternate explanation: someone may simply have placed the German recording for the A-line train onto the B-line. Probably the reverse had happened, too, which meant that wagonloads of German families equipped with water bottles and fanny packs, their kids sporting Mickey ears, had just learned they were en route to the airport.

Either way, the situation demonstrated a problem, and I wondered how it would be addressed.

In France people pride themselves on what is known as the Cartesian Method. It's a kind of problem-solving founded on the principle of suspicion. You start with a hunch that things may not be as simple as they seem, which helps you identify a problem. Then you break it into parts, prioritize the steps of your solution, and march forward in the simplest way possible.

The Cartesian method is fundamentally un-American. I, for instance, address problems the way you might swat at flies, trying to make them go away. The French prefer to dissect the fly. They strive to understand its motives. Then they figure out how to discourage it from pestering you.

I'm not trying to say one method is better than the other. There's a time and a place for each. When my friend Guy spends half an hour studying a wine list in a restaurant, I tend to think the French could do with a little less dissection. On the other hand, when an opportunity for geopolitical intervention presents itself, I feel my own country might do well to resist the swatting impulse.

Because I travel to the airport regularly, I was able to track progress on the announcement problem. A month later I found myself back on the same train, and when we reached the station at the fork, I listened. Passengers who were French, English, or Italian were heading to Charles de Gaulle, but our German fellow voyagers were still traveling to Disneyland. This time no one in my car seemed to care, but as the train started forward, I again noticed several blond people with suitcases standing bemused on the platform.

Clearly the officials in charge hadn't reached the first step of the Method. They didn't yet know there was a problem.

In the course of experiments, I believe scientists should remain simple observers. You don't want them poking at the petri dish, adding their own germs to whatever dread disease they're breeding. But it occurred to me I might put things in motion. On the website of the RATP—the transit authority—I found a page inviting feedback. It bore an invigorating title: *The RATP is listening to you!*

I filled out the form, but when I clicked on the submit button, the link was dead. At first I found this irritating, but then I was impressed with the technology. Haven't we all developed mechanisms for pretending to listen while remaining deaf to suggestions? They had reproduced with exquisite fidelity my own reaction to my wife's suggestion that I "loosen up," or my daughter's recommendation that I "chill out." As artificial intelligence continues to refine its miming of human interactions, we should expect more features of this sort.

So it continued. Many months passed. The B-line trains were still sending Germans scrambling onto the platform, laden with suitcases and duffels. I managed to help one or two, but you couldn't save them all. Sometimes I was frozen with indecision, and when the train clunked into motion, I glided past a row of puzzled faces.

Worse yet, I worried I was seeing the same people again and again. After all, having bailed out of the B-line, wouldn't they simply try the A-train? And then, after a couple days at Disneyland, they'd realize it wasn't an airport, so they'd try the B-line again, setting the whole process back in motion. It had been a long time since I'd read Dante, but I was pretty sure there was a ring of hell just like the RATP.

I tried the website again, and now the submit button worked. I filled out the form and soon received an automated reply assuring me that my input was of the utmost importance. I understood: they had improved their technology and were now able to mechanize a version of the "uh-huhs" that my wife utters during my rants.

Still, it was only a matter of time before they figured it out, and once the problem was identified, the dissection of the fly would begin. But what solution would they cook up? I tried to put myself in Descartes's shoes. Probably they would reverse the recordings, and some poor RATP worker would trudge from the A-line office to the B-line with a thumb drive in his hand. But maybe the corresponding recording had been lost. Then they might have to cut the words "Marne-la-Vallée/Disneyland" from the German tape, splicing in the Italian-accented version of the airport. Or else they'd approach one of the Germans hanging about the train stations—they were so abundant now—and recruit them to re-record it.

Months later, the misdirection continued. I wondered if it was somehow deliberate. After all, history tells us of a longstanding French-German rivalry, and although the RATP isn't known for playing practical jokes, there's always a first time. There was even a chance the recording was part of the government's plan to goose the economy, holding German tourists in the city for an extra day or two.

And then it happened. I was headed to the airport one autumn morning huddled on my seat, drifting at the edge of sleep. The train stopped at the fork, and the announcements began. First came the seductive tones of the woman in French, easing our passage. Next it was the nasal rendition of the upright Brit. Then came the impassioned Italian, reveling in our imminent arrival at Charrrrles de Gaulle.

I held my breath as the silence stretched.

The tone sounded and the doors closed. We tipped into motion.

After nearly two years, the German recording had been cut. They had out-Cartesianed Descartes, finding the simplest solution of them all.

PART THREE

Conquered

Cock-o-Van

SABINE CRACKED OPEN THE DOOR, and the aroma sent me sniffing so hard that my nostrils flattened. Anne, too, craned for a whiff.

Our hostess rolled her eyes to the heavens. "The maestro's hard at work," she grumbled, nodding toward the kitchen. "Striving for greatness."

I found Guy at the stove, the ties of his gray apron snugged in a bow. My friend has floppy hair and a rather prominent nose, so as he wielded his wooden spoon and whisk amidst the pots and pans, he looked a bit like Ringo Starr wrapping up a solo. The smells, though, weren't rock and roll. They were symphonic. Above pungent bass notes of fowl there floated a woodwindy twang of mushrooms, a horn-like complaint of ham, and then, on top of it all, something slender and lyrical that gamboled in the air—an almost citrusy tumble of strings. My mouth watered, and also, somehow, my ears.

"What's he making?" I rasped.

"Peuh!" Sabine spat from behind us. "Another of his crazy ideas. Don't know why he never listens to me."

Guy is hands-down the best cook I know. I've seen him create oxtail stew on a camping stove, and his paella will transport you straight to Valencia. For him, ingredients are everything. He will traverse the city to fetch a rare spice, and in back-alley handoffs he purchases strange animals and rock-hard disks of goat cheese. In a city where lots of people talk the cuisine talk, Guy walks the walk. He doesn't so much *make* meals as *compose* them. I consider him the Frédéric Chopin of gastronomy—as long as you picture Mrs. Chopin nagging him to stop making such a racket. Sabine is undoubtedly the world's most demanding public. Still, Guy approaches his lot in life with good-natured resignation. As an *artiste* he may be under-appreciated, but he is not yet morally defeated.

Our friends' small home is in the outskirts of Paris—filled with books, and decorated with art prints by their son. The meal before us that night was *coq au vin*—a chicken-in-wine-sauce recipe that harks from Guy's ancestral Burgundy. At the dinner table, while the first spoonful melted on my tongue, Sabine wrinkled her nose and began laying out her grievances. First of all, she accused her husband of purism, which meant that he had made the dish with an actual *coq*—that is, a rooster, an animal reputed to be as tough as hippopotamus hide. The fine texture in my mouth now turned a bit chewy, reminding me of the leather of my old tennis shoes, which also happened to be red. Next, Sabine complained how Guy was a stickler for using everything. She counted off the body parts that he'd included here: liver, heart, gizzard, neck—all of it mashed together for extra flavor. The more she detailed the recipe, the more my tongue rebelled. Soon she reached her pièce de résistance, and my throat refused to swallow. Guy had insisted, she said, driving her finger in the air, on stirring gloppy cups of real blood into the sauce.

I stared into my bowl with the distinct impression that it was staring back.

Like many Americans, I have a squeamish relationship with food. Given the tidy presentation of meat and poultry in American grocery stores, it's easy to tell yourself that pork chops and chicken breasts might possibly be harvested in fields, yanked from the dirt like so many potatoes. The steaks I buy in the States are trimmed of bone and fat, remarkably uniform in size, looking comfortably mass-produced. Someday, they say, New York strips and rib eyes will all grow in petri dishes, sprouting overnight like Chia Pets. And if I ignore the pink moisture collecting in the plastic wrap of American meats, I can almost convince myself that this day has arrived, and that I'm more or less a vegan.

In Paris such self-delusion is harder to maintain. My local butcher shop is decorated with fowl of many sorts, and some of the corpses are still partly feathered, usually with heads loosely attached, the yellow beaks gaping in surprise, the tiny black eyes looking out plaintively, as if to say, *Why*

me? Skinned rabbits dangle from meat hooks, along with strings of sausage coiled like garden hose. When I ask for a cutlet or two, a man named Roger wipes red ooze from his hands before grabbing what appears to be a human ribcage. He chats while hacking away. The scene reminds me of Jack Nicholson in *The Shining*.

When Sabine complained about Guy's *coq au vin*, her tastes had for once overlapped with my own preference for keeping the animal out of my animal. Thus an idea was born. Or sprouted. Like a Chia Pet.

Back in the States I'd learned to make a Midwestern version of *coq au vin*—people there pronounced it cock-o-van—a dish that didn't require roosters or blood or gizzards, where brandy replaced cognac, and cheap plonk from California masqueraded as wine. Multiple guests had assured me it was "divine," showing how American ingenuity can take a French idea and make it better, the way we did with photography, the combustion engine, and French fries. Wouldn't Parisians be thrilled to see how their own dish had grown up overseas? It might even crowbar a compliment out of Sabine.

"Are you crazy?" Anne said when I told her of my plan. It was what you call a rhetorical question.

After all, Sabine is famously judgmental. "Just look at his mug," she once said of a new politician. "You can tell he's a crook even before he opens his mouth." She scorns celebrities and has choice words about the weather. If anything needed to be tenderized by stewing in a pot for hours, it was Sabine herself. She represented the ultimate challenge for the American can-do spirit.

Timing, I realized, was everything. We extended the dinner invitation two weeks later—long enough for the gustatory memory of the previous meal to settle but not yet disappear. I didn't announce the menu, mentioning breezily that I'd "whip up something simple." Back in elementary school I'd learned the merit of keeping expectations low.

Thus the trap was laid, and when the day arrived, I went shopping for bait.

Paris is famous for its open-air markets, and three of these lie within easy walking distance of our apartment. My favorite runs along the Boulevard Auguste Blanqui where, three days a week, city workers in green coveralls mantle and dismantle what looks like a long refugee camp. The rickety shelter of tarp-covered poles extends for a full kilometer. On Sundays, half the neighborhood's residents will elbow their way through this gauntlet, placing purchases in straw baskets or packing them around the baby in their stroller. The salespeople wear thick sweaters and, in winter, little woolen gloves with the fingers cut off. Their voices rise above the hubbub as they call out prices and cajolements. Although many stands look similar, people will happily queue up for green beans from their favorite produce vendor rather than buy identical ones from the uncrowded stand next door. I, for instance, never stop at the first Italian food stand, always purchasing ravioli from the dark-haired woman at the second one. I'm not sure that her pasta is any better, but I enjoy her dimples and her sassy ways. This is the key: the open-air market is partly about food, but mostly about relationships.

The markets also bind us to something authentic. Their farm-like aura helps city-dwellers feel connected to the earthiness of *terroir*, to their peasant roots—or even, since many of the products are caked with bits of the farm from which they came, the earthiness of soil itself. For the space of a few hours, we live in the illusion that Paris is a fertile field rather than a never-ending strip of blacktop.

It's only after the market closes and the vendors drive away that a different side of the capital becomes apparent. Before city workers cart away the crates and trash left behind, a population of gleaners emerges from the shadows—old women and vagrants who pick through the detritus, hunting for a partially intact clementine, a cheese in late middle age, or a ball of lettuce as shriveled as the trophy of a Borneo head hunter.

These scenes are always humbling. Back at the time of the French Revolution, gourmet cuisine (or, for that matter, mere eating) was left out of the Declaration of Human Rights, and this seems like a serious oversight. A few decades ago the first *Restos du Coeur*, or Restaurants of the Heart, opened up in Paris, and this chain of soup kitchens has grown more necessary every year. A related problem is what they call *la malbouffe*: bad diet. The French now devour great quantities of processed foods, snacks, sodas, and saturated fats. It's the Americanization of their meals, which has driven their blood sugar to Eiffel Tower heights. And who says French women don't get fat? The typical Parisian silhouette may not yet compete with those trundling through Midwestern shopping malls, but let's not kid ourselves about the direction it's headed.

Probably, it occurred to me, they'd all be better off if they ate more *coq au vin*, or even more cock-o-van.

When the open-air markets aren't running—which happened to be the case today—most people do the bulk of their shopping at supermarkets, many of which are owned by the multinational Carrefour. The near-monopoly has had problematic effects. Over the years the company has worked to elbow name brands off the shelf in favor of generic knock-offs. Instead of a jug of Nutella, why not pick up their delicious Hazelnut-Flavored-Spreading-Paste? Push aside those bottles of Perrier and try out the Naturally-Fizzy-Mineral-Water-with-Tiny-Bubbles. Worse, the packaging of the off-brands is annoyingly familiar, so it's easy to get home and find a container of Humorous-Bovine-Cheese in your bag, when you could have sworn you'd purchased Laughing Cow.

I sometimes go to our neighborhood supermarket, but I stall out in certain sections. Some French restaurants leave you with no choice at all on their menu, but supermarkets tip the scale in the other direction. For example, the ham section of my local store presents no fewer than thirty variations of this meat, requiring you choose between cooked or aged, steamed or baked, plain or salted, thick or thin, with or without the gristly rind. (That last choice seems especially unnecessary.) I am similarly stumped in the yoghurt aisle, where no fewer than fifty alternatives blur behind the glass doors of the cooler.

Of course, my repatriation of *coq au vin* in its improved Midwestern form required that I make do with French rather than American ingredients, so I needed to aim for top-of-the-line. Supermarkets were thus out of the question. This led me to the specialty shops—all those butchers, bakers, and candlestick-makers you find in Paris neighborhoods. At the butcher I ordered several pieces of bird—not rooster, of course, but naturally tender chicken parts that I asked Roger to skin and debone, which is to say, de-animalize. He was also kind enough to chop up tiny Lego-bricks of ham.

When I told him what I was preparing, he lit up. "Oh. But then you'll need some—"

I raised my palms just in time. There was no need to bring up the blood.

Down the street I conferred lengthily with my wine merchant. The bakery supplied a dense loaf I needed for croutons. Then came the *fromagerie*, where I acquired a selection of cheeses that could only be described as heart-stopping—perhaps even literally given the fat content.

On the block where I live there's a produce shop I consider to be a Noah's Ark for fruits and vegetables. If the Great Flood were coming, you'd want a place like this on hand: no giant bins of monoculture, but rather every imaginable species of tomato or lettuce, each represented by a small number of high-quality specimens—enough to repopulate the earth with deliciousness once the waters recede. Here the role of Noah is played by a young man of Algerian descent named Amine, and as I ran down my list that afternoon, he scurried to gather my order of greens, tomatoes, garlic, and mushrooms. Finally it was time for the secret weapon of my recipe, the very backbone of cock-o-van: pearl onions.

Amine looked at me in astonishment. "What?"

It was at that moment that I realized I'd never actually purchased pearl onions in France. Had I ever seen them here? I felt a tightening in my chest.

The pearl variety is not to be confused with dwarfish regular onions, known, not surprisingly, as *petits oignons*. Nor are they the same as green onions (*oignons de printemps*), or—God forbid—shallots (*échalotes*). No, pearl onions go by a different label in France, named after those little spherical bells you find on Christmas ornaments or on the collars of cats—a *grelot*. In the States I could buy these marble-sized onions (usually bound in a tiny net) pretty much anywhere—certainly at the supermarket, probably at the 7-Eleven, and quite possibly from those little creatures who knock at my door selling Girl Scout cookies. The idea that *oignons grelot* could not be had in a Paris shop that basically specialized in onions took me aback.

It was especially puzzling given how prevalent onions are in everyday life in France. I don't just mean onion soup or onion pie, but even their presence outside of cooking. Onions play such an important role in France that the word has become a synonym for the multi-layeredness of one's personal life, as in the expression, "Don't mess with my onions," which is an invitation to keep your nose out of another person's business. Indeed, these vegetables are so primordial that they double as a part of the human body. I discovered this one day in Dr. Pédron's office when I stood in my underwear and he looked down at the bulbous joints of my big toes. "You have onions," he declared, and he didn't mean the pearl kind. It was the French term for bunions. I already have cauliflower ears from roughhousing as a kid, and my barber here refers to a rebellious sprout of my hair as a corn stalk, but now I was starting to feel like one of those Renaissance portraits where the fellow is made of produce.

What to do? I suspected that Guy knew of a black market for rare vegetables, but I wanted to handle it on my own.

There's a temple of shopping on the Left Bank called "Le Bon Marché." It's a vast department store trading largely in luxury goods. *Bon marché* generally means "cheap" or "inexpensive" in French, but in this case the term could only be applied ironically. The elegant four-story structure includes *La Grande Épicerie*—the Louis Vuitton of grocery stores, priced to match. It is my last resort in shopping, but I am now happy to report that if your local shop is out of stock, it's not market day in your neighborhood, and there's no 7-Eleven readily available, it is possible to procure *oignons grelot* at this location. Bring your credit card.

I set to work. Steam billowed. Meat sizzled. Corks popped. I measured, chopped, diced, sliced, peeled, turned, poured, stirred, and spiced, working over the giant pot like the sorcerer's apprentice. By the time I finished, the kitchen was a landscape of peelings, cartons, and pans. But the cock-o-van—roosterless, bloodless, and gizzard-free—bubbled gently, pearl onions rising occasionally to the surface like so many eyeballs. In celebration, I put on some music. It was Chopin.

Whereas Guy had served us strips of shoe leather, my pot contained succulent morsels of heaven. The chicken was beefy red on the outside, but it fell apart at the slightest touch, the innards virginally white. A small spice bundle floated in the thickening sauce, and concentrated Côtes du Rhône had begun to etherize me. When I sipped at my wooden spoon, the room danced. Somehow the local ingredients had enhanced it. My Midwesternized version of the French dish had improved with its re-importation.

It's not often that I pull off a coup of this sort, but for once the hunter-gatherer who lived inside me had risen to the occasion, plucking foods at the apex of tastiness and transforming them into earthly paradise. Sabine would have no idea what hit her. In terms of shock value, the meal would surpass the German lightning campaign of 1939, when tanks skirted the Maginot Line and parked at people's doorsteps.

Steam misted the window. Both the pot and I bubbled happily.

The doorbell rang, and Anne went to answer. Greetings ensued, followed by the shuffle of feet on the mat. Jackets came off, and Guy's voice rose. It smelled great, he was saying, and he wanted to know what I had made. Anne made the mistake of telling him.

"Peuh!" Sabine spat. "You've got to be kidding. I was hoping for Tex-Mex."

War of the Worlds

IT WAS ONE OF THOSE SPRING-LIKE AFTERNOONS, and I'd emerged from a restaurant in the sixth arrondissement. Since our daughter's school wouldn't release her for another hour, I had time to take in the surroundings. Voices spilled from the terrace café at the corner, and an old man tugged a terrier by his leash. Over at the bakery, four armor-clad riot police (known locally as the CRS) waited their turn to order pastries. A fifth one stood guard outside, holding their shields and watching out for the brass.

Then I noticed they were not alone. The less peckish among them—forty or so—formed a bulwark a block away, where, I now realized, a mob of protesters paraded along the cross street. Placards and banners bobbed against the background of shop signs.

As I strained to make out their chorus of chants, a volley of air horns cut through it all, triggering a symphony of police whistles. Then a bang sounded—the way you might ask your percussionist to wallop his kettle drum at a critical moment. A cloud unfurled upward in the sky. The air went peppery.

No doubt about it: I was a cobblestone's throw from a mass demonstration—*une manifestation*, or more colloquially, *une manif*.

Despite the tumult, the cops at the bakery still dithered over éclairs and brownies. So, in my relentless pursuit of knowledge, I approached the old man with the dog. He stood at the edge of the sidewalk as his terrier hunched in the gutter, scooting his hind feet forward as though trying to seat himself on an invisible stool.

"*Qu'est-ce qui se passe?*" I said while the demonstrators skirmished half a block away.

The man studied me, his eyes heavy with the wisdom of the ages. "*Il chie,*" he declared, stating it like one of those expressions for the weather: *it is raining, it is snowing*—and now, of all things, *it is shitting.*

It sounded like cultural commentary, but then I noticed the tawny pile in the gutter. Lightened of his terrible load, the dog now led his master down the street, both of them oblivious to the cries and the clouds of tear gas.

As history teaches us, some people are freedom fighters and others are collaborators—but most just want to get on with the business of life.

Manifs—which sometimes turn violent—go with the territory around here. France is famous for its commitment to authority and order, but every so often the top blows off the mountain and you're left with a volcanic cauldron of revolution.

It's tempting to imagine the country as composed of two groups—rabble-rousers facing off against disciplinarians—but things aren't so simple. Both impulses infect each person, expressing themselves on alternate days. Your run-of-the-mill Parisian is the sort of monster Dr. Frankenstein might have contrived if his choice for body parts had been limited to Louis XVI and Robespierre—that is, the limbs of total domination and total revolution. Stitched together, they form a creature whose main activity consists of smacking himself.

If you had recently teleported to Paris from Mars—or, for that matter, from the US—such scenes of civil unrest would be cause for concern. *WTF?* you might say (or whatever the Martian equivalent is). It would appear to you that civilization had reached a point of no return, and that France might soon be up for grabs by neighboring countries (or planets).

However, hang around for a while, and you figure out this isn't a scene of group insanity. Mass protest is such a common form of misbehavior here that Parisians face demonstrations the way a Minnesotan greets blizzards—you grit your teeth and trudge into it. In Paris there are often multiple blizzards at the same time (on a good day you might have eight or ten to choose from), so an industry of websites has emerged to keep us abreast of the social climate. A quick check tells where the day's demonstrations are set to begin and at what time, how many trade unions will be on strike, which services will be shut down, and even—to make sure the processions don't bump into each other on especially popular days—which routes the protesting mobs plan to follow.

No one knows how many demonstrators show up at these events. The nightly news provides a police tally, followed by the competing claims of the organizers. The police estimate is always surprisingly low, as if they have a hard time counting on their fingers because of those bulky gloves. However, the unions' figures are only plausible if demonstrators are also nesting dolls, each one containing a set of progressively smaller picketers inside. The truth is, as we so often find these days, up for grabs.

Today's procession was on the larger side, one of those million-person marches (maybe half that, if you counted like the police), and it had an unruly quality. Sometimes the mood of a demonstration is described as *bon enfant*— easy-going, even slightly jolly, with the protesters having a bit of fun as they bring traffic to its knees. This group was less bubbly. The evening news presenters would almost certainly call it *turbulent*.

Just now another bang sounded, touching off a series of whoops. I couldn't see through the mass of bodies, but somewhere glass shattered, and a car alarm went off. Was it possible they'd go the next step and start lighting vehicles on fire? The festive roasting of Renaults and Citroens reaches a peak in France on New Year's Eve, but occasionally the locals engage in this pastime during the warmer months, too.

With Anne out of town, I was on pickup duty. Our daughter's school wasn't that far away, but many roads were now blocked, and several Metro stations had wisely closed their doors. So, I availed myself of one of those public bicycles—a clunky Vélib with a skipping chain—and pedaled along side streets, weaving between the rock that was the riot police and the hard place of the throng.

Back in the US, we have our share of demonstrations, but they tend to be, for lack of a better term, wimpier. Americans might take to the streets for a day or two, but they can't match the work ethic of those French men and women who, every morning, don their uniform of protest and trudge dutifully to the picket lines. The participation rates are staggering. Adjusting for population, a Parisian-scale protest would equal six million descending on Washington, which happens once every never. It's not as if Americans have run short of reasons for mutiny. It's just hard to get them out of the house. After all, the next episode on Netflix is always about to auto-start, so we put off full-fledged rebellion for another twenty-two minutes.

Sadly, I'm as bad as the rest of them. When I'm stateside, the resident protesters in my Midwestern town are three aging hippies who have dedicated their golden years to waving signs at motorists from the town square. Because they understand the effort it would take for people to park their car and join them, their placards aim for more modest participation. *Honk for #MeToo*, they read. *Honk if Black Lives Matter. Honk to Stop Global Warming.*

I wave back and—because I usually believe in their cause—I give a toot. It's quite literally the least I could do, and a kind of glumness settles on me every time my horn peters into silence. When I get home, I'll click to donate a few bucks, but the gesture feels cheap, even cowardly—the way, long ago, you could buy your way out of the army by paying someone to take your place.

In Paris, on the other hand, I have become civically engaged. My friends Guy and Sabine are hearty militants—the kind who, whenever a little free time presents itself, check out the available demonstrations the way one might browse through movie listings. When they find something that appeals, I will often tag along, marching in the streets to condemn the new education reform or the salary cuts, protesting the *this* or the *that*, helping to swell (to different degrees, of course) the official or unofficial count of protesters.

Some years ago, I purchased a T-shirt with a blood-red NON! printed across the chest. This proved to be a great all-purpose accessory for demonstrations of every flavor. For a while, I looked for a matching OUI! shirt, in order to be prepared for all circumstances. Turns out there's no call for such a thing. People regularly protest against, but rarely for.

Often demonstrations are paired with strikes, another local specialty. Americans used to walk off the job, too, but after the '70s, interest flagged. A daylong strike is headline news in the US, whereas here it's business as usual. In Western Europe, the French are the undisputed champs of not getting anything done, beating the Germans fourteen-fold.

Another website tracks these work stoppages (at least when the web technicians themselves aren't on strike), which tend to be vast and tectonic. Shutdowns screech whole sectors of the economy to a standstill, and sometimes we are treated to fine spectacles—things like truckloads of hay being dumped on the Champs-Elysées, or yellow-vested protesters lighting bonfires on some of the squares.

It's like those scenes from science fiction movies, the ones where great cities are reduced to fire and rubble by the Z-rays and finger-bolts of the Martian invaders. Only in this case, the extraterrestrials can just lean back and watch the Earthlings do all the work themselves.

Huffing along side streets on my bike, I popped out now and then to see if the crowd had thinned. But no, it was even larger now. At the intersection with the Boulevard Saint-Michel, the police had amassed a fleet of vans and paddy wagons, where officers channeled protesters along an allowed itinerary.

The air was now hazy with tear gas and smoke. I rolled to a stop in front of an officer sitting on the bumper of his vehicle. He was hunched over, staring at his boots. When I asked where I might cross the churning river of people, he looked up to reveal a patch of gauze taped over his eye. Evidently people had started throwing things. The poor cyclops waved me wordlessly toward the east.

In the old days, cobblestones were the tool of choice for protesters. They made for effective projectiles. Moreover, you could heap them into barricades against the royalists, the national guard, or whoever happened to be the enemy *du jour*. Then, a hundred and fifty years ago, folks cut wide boulevards through the city, making the barricades harder to build. These days people mostly hurl chunks of blacktop. It may not have the historic brio of cobblestones, but it's easier to chip up.

The crowd marched with flags and banners, and some demonstrators anchored helium balloons bearing union logos. One young man wearing a red vest and wrap-around sunglasses brandished a burning traffic flare in a Statue-of-Liberty sort of pose.

In peaceful times, Parisians tend to walk in a straight-backed and self-contained manner, as if someone had pressed the barrel of a revolver to their back and ordered them to move forward without any funny business. During *man-ifs*, however, this corporeal discipline dissolves. Protesters lumber. They develop swagger. Suddenly the whole street belongs to them, and they try to fill it. In short, they start walking like Americans.

At this point I'd cycled northeast in search of clear passage, skirting the Latin Quarter. In this area, tourists lounged at terrace cafés and calm reigned supreme. Sightseeing is a multi-billion-dollar industry here, so the government shoos protesters away from popular locations. The official tourism website never speaks of "demonstrations." It refers to events like this as "public disturbances"—making them sound like block parties that have turned a bit exuberant, rather than a great collective retching.

In the US, shopkeepers would tack plywood over their storefronts on a day like this. Survivalists would oil their assault rifles. There'd be a run on batteries and toilet paper. But in Paris, people shrug. Even though Armageddon was going down a couple blocks away, the greatest nuisance at the café was trying to catch your waiter's eye so you could order another round.

What, I wondered, would a Martian visitor make of this situation? Probably it would leave him scratching both his heads.

I checked my watch. By this point, I'd cycled nearly to the river. The broad avenue was still clogged with protesters. I'd been expecting things to thin out, the way a serpent narrows after the bulge of a swallowed rat. But there was no bulge—or rather, there was nothing *but* bulge, as if the snake had actually swallowed its own tail, forming an endless loop of protesters. The TV news anchors would announce the size of the demonstration as *infinite*. The unions would giggle with glee.

There were more bangs and clouds of smoke. Overhead came the *thup-thup-thup* of a helicopter, the sign that things were getting out of hand. A little squadron of riot police trotted past me bearing stub-barreled guns. We were now reaching the Flash-Ball stage—those rubber bullet weapons designed to keep the mob at bay. They looked like stormtroopers. Pretty soon I'd have Darth Vader bearing down on me, wheezing in that special way he has, as if he needs a throat lozenge.

I was now in the neighborhood where my friend Cécile lived, so I pulled out my phone and gave her a ring. She was still at work.

"*Qu'est-ce qui se passe?*" she said.

I thought of the answer the dog owner had given me nearly an hour ago. *Il chie*, I wanted to say. *It's shitting out.* But instead I took a picture with my phone and sent it. It showed fifty riot police standing in rank, plastic shields raised, as if ready to charge.

"*Merde*," she commented. "I have to pick up Matthieu and Maryse from school. How am I supposed to get there?"

Everyone had the same problem. Down one of the calmer streets, an elementary school had already opened its doors, releasing a herd of children. Eight-, nine-, and ten-year-olds gawked at the bedlam before them. A girl in a pleated blue skirt held her father's hand while studying the commotion with a knit brow, her lips pursed with disapproval.

What, I had to wonder, would she learn from this scene?

French children of this age are the opposite of revolution. While American kids clown around and squirm in their seats, their French counterparts learn discipline. Starting in first grade they practice sitting straight for long stretches, controlling not just their bodies, but even their minds. They learn moral tales by heart—edifying rhymes about how much better it is to be a workaday ant than a tuneful cicada, or how crows will drop their camembert if they talk with their mouth full. All is order.

Then these kids enter the cocoon of middle school and emerge as revolutionaries, eager to take down the man and earn their freedom. While American high schools work to let every flower bloom, French students experience education as *The Shawshank Redemption*.

I pushed off from the curb and pedaled onward, hoping to loop past the great serpent of protest. If necessary, I'd go as far as the Place de la Bastille—which is, after all, where the ancestors of these protesters cut their eyeteeth in 1789.

The helicopter *thup-thupped* more distantly now, and the air-horn blasts were muffled. The road tipped downhill and I wheeled past a block of tall buildings, veering onto an empty boulevard. Yellow garlands of police ribbon still stretched across the side streets, and a haze of smoke hung in the air. Beyond the curve to the west, chanting voices dwindled. Cans and bottles clogged the gutters. Trade union flags lay abandoned.

The snake of the mob had finally passed, leaving nothing but droppings. It had shat.

Then came a rumble from the far end of the street, and the ground began to shudder. Veiled by wisps of smoke, a tall vehicle appeared, followed by another. Hydraulics whined, and a little green man walked out of the haze. He wielded a wand with a tube unspooling from its hilt like the hose of a flamethrower or, perhaps, a plasma-ray. A second green figure joined him, similarly armed. And then a third.

This was how I'd imagined it going down—otherworldly creatures emerging from their craft, ready to mop up the remains of the human race. They'd bided their time, but now the extraterrestrials were making their move.

Clouds of white billowed from their weapons. Leaflets and bottles jumped forward along their path. And voices rang out, heavily accented, although not with that trademark Martian twang. Turned out, these were aliens of a different sort—immigrants, men charged with the job of cleaning up behind an outraged citizenry, and whose own children attended school somewhere in the capital, learning the art of civil disobedience.

Which reminded me of my daughter. By now, she'd have been released into the brutal classroom of life.

Right on cue, a text from her arrived with a picture of riot police near her school, shields raised, truncheons at the ready, a background of smoke and armored vehicles. It looked like an invasion.

How would she take it? I'd have all that comforting to do, once we got home. After wiping away her tears, I'd explain what I could about violence and unrest, about struggles for power. I'd make up soothing reassurances. With a fatherly shoulder-scrunch, I'd buck my daughter up, and after a bowl of chicken soup, I would tuck her—

The phone buzzed again. Her caption appeared in a single word. "AWESOME."

I sighed. It was worse than I'd imagined: our little girl was becoming French.

Underground Man

By the time we rendezvoused near the Metro station, I'd already fiddled the scene into the start of a screenplay. There'd be Gilles (French, mustachioed, clad in blue coveralls), and an American named...I don't know...maybe *Trent*. Yes, that would do nicely. He'd be a square-jawed thirty-something, wearing a safari shirt and cargo pants, a leather satchel slung over his shoulder. The two protagonists would steal into the shadows, Gilles drawing a crowbar from his bag. Soon a manhole cover would clatter to the side and blackness would gape. A trickle of water would echo in the darkness, followed by the squeak of rodents. At that point Gilles would shrink back. But Trent? No. He'd stride ahead, lowering himself down the tooth-like rungs, disappearing into the gullet.

Well, it ended up being sort of like that. But also, sort of not. We *were* on a Paris street, and I *did* have cargo pants on—the cuffs of which I'd tucked into my socks for the sake of tidiness. Beyond that, the wretched machine that passes for my imagination was spinning cotton candy. In the imaginary screenplay, I'd spared Trent the crimson garden gloves I currently wore, as well as the duct tape sling I'd arts-and-crafted to tote my water bottle. Right now a battery-powered lamp was strapped to my forehead, but that wouldn't work for the movie. Heroes enter caverns brandishing a torch, of course. And maybe I'd give Trent a bullwhip. Or maybe not. You don't want to be over-the-top.

We were still on the sidewalk when Gilles nudged me from this reverie, pointing toward the hole. "OK. You first."

I peered down. "Are you kidding?" I said. What was he thinking? I mean, you couldn't even see the bottom—at least, not unless you got a lot closer to the edge than this particular Trent was planning to go.

Cut! the director in my brain shouted. *End of scene!*

But then the shaming about my manhood began, and before I knew it I was laddering my way down, knocking my elbows on the sides of the shaft. Every twenty feet or so I passed through a circular landing the size of a submarine hatch. Grit rained down, and when I looked up, Gilles was entering too, silhouetted against the shrinking circle of sky. Metal scraped again, and the lid clattered back in place, a total eclipse.

The rungs ended. I had boots on the ground, seven stories beneath the pavement. Trent would have squared his fedora and soldiered on. Whereas me, I waited for my guide and my breath to catch up, taking a moment to reflect on how I'd landed here.

For years I'd been chasing an idea, trying to plumb the Paris-ness of Paris, grilling the city like a detective, probing it like a psychiatrist. What, I wanted to know, was it all about?

One possibility: Paris was just the sum of its eccentricities. The other: there was a kernel somewhere, an irreducible nub that explained the city's neurosis with the clarity of a childhood trauma. I wanted to know its problem, the dirty little secrets that lay at its heart. But the city's defense mechanisms are too strong. *I am fine*, Paris always protests. *Indeed, better than fine. I am…superb.*

Which explains the grand airs. Everyone knows how the theaters sparkle in Paris, how the domes glint, and the monuments swagger. Street names honk of Napoleonic victories, and even your subway map could double as a history lesson. More glamorous than the Louvre that it contains, Paris becomes the museum of itself, putting its curves on display and swooning over its own image, mirrored in the eyes of its admirers.

Why, I have wondered, can't Paris be more humble, more gracious, more, well…Midwestern? In my part of the States, even when we toot our own horn we make sure to add a few flat notes. For every Kennedy Boulevard, you want a Taft Avenue or a Millard Fillmore Cul-de-sac, just to take you down a peg or two.

The problem is the glitz. Every time you get a whiff of poverty in Paris, the aroma of luxury rolls in and overwhelms you. The squabbling of religions is drowned out by church bells. Prostitution gets ushered behind the curtain of romance and cancan girls. Everything seedy and unsavory is clamped beneath a lid policed by the tourist bureau.

There had to be some way to go deeper, to get to the bottom of it.

I'd been noodling this idea one day while a jackhammer chattered outside my window. Down the street, three men had laid out orange cones. By the end of the afternoon, they were knee-deep in the road. The next day, they were up to their hips. After that, the big machinery rolled in—tank-trucks with tentacles of stout hose, gray slime oozing from the fittings. Then a sign appeared, announcing: *Consolidation Des Sols*—a Shoring Up of the Ground. The words sent my eyebrows airborne. I'd been snooping on the surface of the city, but perhaps the real drama was going on *underground*. A new idea sprang to mind: Paris wasn't Gigi or Amélie Poulain. No, it was Jules Verne and *Journey to the Center of the Earth*.

My spine tingled. Was that an adventure blowing in my ear? The idea of Trent was born.

To learn about the bottom of the city, I called my friend Charles-Albert and invited him to lunch. As an architect, he was paid to know things.

"Paris is a Swiss cheese," he explained between spoonfuls of eggplant gazpacho. "A Swiss cheese infested by maggots. It's amazing that anything still stands."

"But what's the *consolidation des*—"

"I'm getting to that."

But he didn't. At least, not right away. Instead, he talked about the 100 miles of subway tunnels crisscrossing the city, the underground garages, the crypts. Not to mention, he continued, the thousands of kilometers of sewer, a subterranean river or two, the millions of utility lines. All of it snaked through the ground, leaving Paris riddled with cavities, on the verge of collapse.

"Yes, but—"

He raised a finger to stop me. Did I know about the twelve hundred kilometers of pneumatic conduits, the ones that used to whoosh messages between post offices? He mentioned access tunnels, wine cellars, naturally formed voids.

"And then," he said, "there are the catacombs. That's the real danger."

I straightened in my seat.

Like almost everyone in Paris, I'd visited the catacombs, back when I was a kid. There's a public entrance over at Denfert-Rochereau, and for a modest fee you clomp down a hundred steps till you reach ghoulish chambers filled with human remains. A couple centuries ago, after local cemeteries started leaking into the water table, the bones of six million Parisians were transported here, assembled in decorative stacks. Whole galleries were dedicated to skulls and femurs. Plaques bore sobering inscriptions about mortality. I recalled how my younger self had halted before an adolescent skull, its clenched grin frozen for eternity. Probably the poor kid had clowned around a lot when he was alive. Maybe he'd never finished his homework on time. There was a good chance he'd been afraid of the dark. And look what became of him!

"The part you visited," Charles-Albert was saying as he shoveled in lunch, "that's just the beginning." He was talking now about the ancient limestone quarries. Like the old legend of pelicans plucking meat from their own breast to feed their young, Paris had been built with stone ripped from the ground beneath it. Hundreds of years ago, the city had literally undermined itself, leaving behind a welter of galleries and shafts—nearly three hundred kilometers worth.

"The truck you saw the other day," he said, "that was one of the city crews. They pump in cement when they worry a building might collapse."

It wasn't lost on me that the *consolidation des sols* was taking place outside my own living room window. I pictured my apartment building crumbling in slow motion, vanishing into a sinkhole the size of a lunar crater. At roughly the same time it occurred to me that Anne was at home—probably reading, or perhaps matching socks still warm from the dryer. I considered calling her with a heads-up. But then I imagined how her eyes would roll and decided to give the warning a rain-check.

Nevertheless, my pulse had quickened. No matter the risk, I knew I needed to dive beneath the shiny surface of this city, exploring its dark meanders. I had hit upon something essential. This was it. Or rather, this was *id*, the opaque center of the city's desire—its drive, its urge, its unconscious.

Who, I wondered, would play me in the movie? Harrison Ford was too old. Bogart was too dead. Maybe Daniel Craig?

Then, just as quickly, the plan stalled.

Turns out no one's allowed in this other part of the catacombs. Going in is illegal, which means you can only get there by connecting with a vaguely criminal underworld. But I'd moled my way into every other aspect of French life, so why not this one? I reached out to my network of friends, asking them to reach out to *their* networks, after which we let the networks network.

People who prowl through the old quarries are known as *cataphiles* (although women are sometimes called *cata-filles*). However, there's also an opposing group of *cata-flics* (cata-cops)—folks charged with keeping you out. The process is tricky, for as soon as you reach out to a member of the secret society of cataphiles, they suspect you may be a cata-cop trying to infiltrate their ranks. So it's best to be inducted by a friend.

Problem was, no one in my circles knew any cataphiles. Several years ago the police had cracked down, welding shut the entrances to the tunnels. These days only a happy few knew how to get in, and finding one of them was like angling for an introduction to the Illuminati.

I'd worked all the channels and run out of leads, was on the brink of giving up. Then one morning a message pinged in my inbox. It consisted of a single line: *Voilà, mettons-nous d'accord*—roughly translated as "let's work something out." The email address consisted of two first names, and at the bottom there stood a phone number, a platoon of straight-backed digits ready to serve. Somewhere in Paris a man awaited my call. I dialed.

Before agreeing to a rendezvous, Gilles quizzed me over the phone about my motives. He was worried I was a spy. I'd seen enough movies to know how these encounters work. Every time the freedom fighters get a new recruit, they need to make sure the guy's not just a German in disguise. Sometimes they rely on passwords or secret codes, and when that's not available, a little torture can be handy—sticking a fork in the guy's thigh to see what language he uses for screaming. When in doubt, a bullet to the head will do the trick. Better safe than sorry.

The time came for a meet, and while pacing on a square in the center of town, I put the finishing touches on the character of Trent. He'd be tall, of course. With chiseled looks. I also decided to give him a tragic past, since a vulnerable hero is more endearing. Meanwhile, I tried not to look up at the buildings around me. I figured Gilles was watching from an upper-story window, scanning the square with high-powered binoculars (or, better, a rifle scope) to make sure I'd come alone.

When finally he appeared, I had to squint to fit him into the dramatic mold I'd prepared. He was a lanky fellow with unblinking eyes, his upper lip sporting a brush-like mustache reminiscent of Thompson and Thomson in *Tintin*. Though verging on middle age, he walked with the casual slump of an American middle schooler.

Our exchange started the way fencers tap their foils to take each other's measure. "So," I began, "how often do you go down there?"

His eyes widened with innocence. "Down *where?*" he parried. It was the kind of answer you give when you're pretty sure the other person wants you to enunciate the words "heroin" and "cash only" into their lapel.

What followed was a conversation as coy as a Midwestern courtship. Two hours later, we still hadn't gotten past the hand-holding stage. By the end of the afternoon Gilles left it up in the air as to whether he'd call again, and for days I waited by the phone like a teenage girl hoping for a second date.

But he did call, making me drop everything for an impromptu meeting. When I showed up, he uttered cryptic phrases, asking if I was "ready," never showing surprise or emotion. Then he led me through a maze of streets, up the steps to an old hospital, along a corridor, across a vast courtyard, into a side building, through a code-protected door, and down an endless flight of stairs, deeper and deeper, until finally we entered a rocky tunnel. It was a civilized stretch of the ancient quarries, now maintained by a private club of white-whiskered old men. Several of them were present, working with pickaxes and wheelbarrows as they turned a hundred meters of underground passageway into a kind of museum, complete with spotlights, placards, construction models, and even mannequins frozen in poses of tunnel-digging. I got the tour. Then we drank our mead-like lunch with the workers, sitting at a table hewn from stone. It was like a congress of dwarves who were hiding from their wives.

This was a start, but it was far from the scenes of danger I'd imagined for my cinematic alter ego. Trent wouldn't twiddle his thumbs in such a small and doctored portion of the quarries. His role called for poisoned darts and treasure. Snakes would be a welcome addition.

"That's it for today," Gilles reported as we returned to the surface.

"But when will we—?"

"I'll give you a call," he said. "Maybe."

When finally his message came, I had less than a day to outfit myself. Gloves and boots were de rigueur, but mostly I worried about light. Gilles had told me the story of Philibert Aspairt, the patron saint of cataphiles—a fellow who lost his way in the tunnels when his lantern went out, and wasn't found till eleven years later. At least, parts of him. So I decided to follow the NASA principle of triple redundancy. In addition to the headlamp, I packed a pocket flashlight, as well as my iPhone. And then, because even NASA sometimes blows things up, I went the quadruple route and purchased a keychain with a tiny penlight fob, one just bright enough to reveal any key-holes we might encounter.

My obsession with light—and perhaps now is the time to confess this—came from a rather longstanding fear of the dark. As a kid I insisted on leaving my door open while I slept, a habit which I have never fully outgrown. I feared the catacombs might not be equipped with Winnie-the-Pooh nightlights. Ordinarily such character flaws would disqualify a person from underground exploration. That said, my fear of darkness was vastly overshadowed by a more commanding form of terror—namely, claustrophobia. At first, the Trent in me thought the two fears might cancel each other out. After all, if you can't even see how the walls of a tunnel are closing in around you, what's there to be afraid of? But more and more I found myself thinking of "The Cask of Amontillado," that Poe story where a man of Gilles-like inscrutability walls his companion into a wine cellar.

Which made me wonder. How much did I really know about Gilles? I added a small penknife to my gear. It included several weapons in addition to the tiny blade: a nail file, a toothpick, and a miniature tweezers.

All this led to the Sunday morning when Gilles and I met in a deserted street. He crow-barred up a manhole cover, and as I climbed down the metal rungs, a repertoire of adventure films flicked through my imagination—not to mention old stories about tunnels, like that one with Theseus in the labyrinth, sword in hand, ready to confront the Minotaur.

Which is what made me realize that Trent, in the movie version, would at this juncture tear at his safari shirt. He'd loosen a thread and tie it to a rung. Its unraveling would provide a guide for his safe return. Better yet, each step would remove a line of fabric, gradually revealing the rippedness of Trent's pecs, baring them in proportion to the growing danger.

"Ready?" Gilles said. He'd joined me at the bottom of the shaft.

I'd managed to turn my headlamp on, and the beam of light played over rough ground, petering into darkness. Rocky passageways branched in two directions. An old beer can lay at my feet.

Gilles struck out to the right, and I scrambled to follow.

Your imagination builds models of dank and cobwebby grottoes, but in fact the quarries are disappointingly clean and crafted. Sometimes they grow wider than your outstretched arms, while at other moments you find your elbows knocking at the sides. Crouching is occasionally required, but often a tall-ish American can walk upright beneath stone ceilings crazed with cracks, bowing with the weight of the metropolis.

"Look here," Gilles said, tapping at a stone in the wall. A series of numbers and letters had been chiseled in—a code showing the year a team had come through to shore up this area in the 1780s, adding masonry supports to keep the city from sinking. Back in the twelfth century, when folks dug out stone for places like Notre-Dame, the galleries followed a vein of limestone less than four feet thick. Quarrymen had labored on hands and knees to extract blocks with chisels and hammers. Then they rolled slabs of stone toward the open shafts, where men in hamster wheels winched them to the surface.

At first the quarries had been private affairs—the way you might decide to dig a gold mine in your backyard. Scores of open shafts pitted the city back then, and they were family businesses. Each quarry was separate—the tunnels not connected. When ceilings collapsed on the fathers, the next generation took over. After a few centuries of excavation, the foundation of Paris turned into a game of Jenga—one where too many pieces had been removed. When whole buildings started to crumble into cavities, enough was enough. In the eighteenth century the city sent in its engineers. At that point there were too many tunnels to fill them up again, so workers scraped the dirt floors down to bedrock and built retaining walls. Small quarries were linked by way of new passageways, and larger caverns were propped with pillars. Eventually everything was connected, forming the world's largest rabbit warren.

Gilles and I had gone down a particularly tight passage when the vibration began. It turned into a rumble, louder and louder. Dust drifted down from the ceiling. In Trent's world it would have meant a chasm was about to open or a boulder would roll toward you; at the very least there'd be some lumbering creature—half man, half bull.

Gilles lifted his head, and his mustache twitched. "Line Six," he said.

It was the Metro rolling forty feet overhead. The bedrock got the shivers every ten minutes, and each line had its own melody.

"Off we go." He plunged ahead. We banked left and right. The walls narrowed, and the floor sloped. We were going down, moving toward the center, to the heart.

What you find in the catacombs is the residue of the past. The walls are covered with scratchings: love notes, obscene drawings, I-was-here signatures, some dating back two hundred years or more. It's a history of the city, preserved in graffiti. Faded stencils announced the pig and horse markets that used to lie overhead on the surface. Street names appeared, though their surface equivalents had long ago vanished or been relabeled. In one section, shreds of electrical wiring remained from WWII, where the German occupiers had set up an underground command post. A scrawled message in another section showed where huddled Parisians took refuge during the nighttime bombing of the Renault factories in March of 1943.

The public part of the catacombs was filled with bones, but here we just elbowed our way through a crowd of ghosts. The silence wasn't even interrupted by the hiss of vipers.

Soon we were sloshing through thigh-deep water. Gilles led me deeper, and the labyrinth narrowed and branched. At this point, in the movie version, the music would start to grow weird and loud—drumbeats, perhaps, or the screeches of a poorly tuned violin. By now, Trent's shirt would be unraveling into ribbons. He'd be ready for the face-off, preferably one that included a chase scene, ideally on runaway mining carts. To my right, a depression in the soil looked like a hoof print.

The tight passage suddenly widened. We found ourselves in a small gallery, and I could breathe again. While snacking on energy bars, we clicked off the headlamps to save batteries, and I found myself in the kind of darkness I'd not experienced since early childhood—a syrupy, choking blackness, the monster-filled kind, where anything can happen, and where, if it did, no one would hear a peep of it.

Gilles's voice rose from the dark. "You tell anyone what you were doing today?"

Why on earth would I have done that? Telling Anne would have led to a discussion about my mental health. And my daughter? She'd have snapped on a headlamp and insisted on coming along.

"No," I said. "Should I have?"

He chuckled, and the hairs on the back of my neck struggled to attention. You always think the Minotaur lies deep within the maze, but what if he's your guide—that fellow you know next to nothing about, to whom you've entrusted your life, who is bigger than you and basically untraceable, and who likes playing the mystery man? I fumbled in my pocket for the penknife. I'd never tweezered a man to death before, but I had a plan: go for the mustache.

Sitting in the darkness, Gilles opened up. He'd been coming into the quarries for years, he said, had even written a book about them. He knew all the clandestine groups of spelunkers who'd mapped the crannies, people who referred to each other by code names and untraceable email addresses. They updated the hand-drawn maps each time a passage collapsed, or when the *consolidation des sols* folks pumped in cement to save the world of the surface. Over the years these quarries had seen it all: noblemen hiding from the guillotine during the Revolution, Parisians taking shelter from air raids, members of the Resistance circumventing Nazis, lovers seeking darkness. Murders had been committed here, bodies found, manhunts launched. People had fallen in pits or been trapped under rocks. The authorities tried to tighten the lid, but the cataphiles always found a new way in. The real problem, he said, was getting out.

We pressed on. The air was warmer now, more humid. Gilles made me squirm through a passage the width of a chubby cat, after which came more water, deeper. We were going down, down. This was it. We were approaching the beginning, the source, the origin.

His headlamp started to blink. It had been six hours, and his batteries were dying. He shrugged. Gilles hadn't bothered with redundancy of the quadruple kind. Probably he could feel his way out. "Don't worry," he said behind his mustache. "If we get separated, I'll come back for you." He left a beat. "In eleven years."

How deep had we gone? The water kept rising. Probably we'd end up in the Seine itself—or perhaps in that dark pool beneath the opera house, where the phantom lived. This was the Underworld, the land of shades. Like Orpheus, I was ready for my revelation.

Gilles tapped me on the shoulder.

"OK," he said. "Up you go."

To our right was another ladder of rungs, disappearing into shadows above.

I climbed and climbed. Then the cover opened and I heaved myself out. From somewhere there came the coo of pigeons, the rumble of a bus. I looked about, half-blinded by daylight.

No, it wasn't the crypt of Notre-Dame or the dungeon of the Conciergerie. It wasn't the pyramid of the Louvre. There were trees overhead, and a busy road buzzed not far away. We were standing between a warehouse and a discount supermarket.

We hadn't ended up in the center at all. No, we'd traveled to the very edge of town, as far from the core as you could get. Somehow the journey to the heart of Paris had ended up at the city's extremities.

"There you go," Gilles said. "That's it for today." He brushed himself off, peeled his gloves from his hands, and

snapped them into a pocket of his coveralls. After confirm-
ing plans for our next excursion, he twitched his mustache
and offered a two-fingered salute, striding off with a bounc-
ing gait.

What had just happened? I'd been wanting to lift the
veil on Paris's secret life, to glimpse its innermost desires. I'd
hoped for something essential—maybe shameful and dirty.
What I'd found instead was emptiness. A presence that was
sturdy, but hollow.

Somehow it reminded me of Millard Fillmore.

On the way home I limped from a sore knee, and my shoes squelched. In a dark shop window I caught a glimpse of my reflection. The man before me had known better times. His cargo pants were torn, and grit clotted his hair. It was all for the best that he hadn't tied that thread to the ladder rung, unraveling the shirt. The fellow before me wasn't quite as ripped as Trent.

Then, of course, it started to pour, and because it hadn't occurred to me that the end of an adventure might require anything as mundane as an umbrella or a wallet or Metro tickets, I started the hike home, the rain melting mud from my legs as if I were a walking statue in a state of rapid decomposition.

I'd dug down to the heart of the city, to its origins, its womb, but what had I found? Not even a plaque or a monument. No center or source. All I had to show for it was bewilderment.

Who knows? Maybe that's the essence of Paris: it keeps you turning, confronts you with yourself, always leaving you a touch off balance.

Too Soon, Too Close

IN RECENT YEARS, people have been trying to blow up my adopted city. Call me intolerant, but frankly it's pissing me off. I guess the schoolgirls who skip past my building twice a day have turned into someone's idea of the enemy. So has our Portuguese concierge, as he rolls out the trash bins, or my Algerian barber, who leans in the doorway of his shop, wiping his hands on a towel. Even the bakery ladies probably stand for all that's gone wrong in the gooey éclair of Western society. The terrorists plan to take them all out.

Mind you, I get it. We're all guilty of something. But maybe not quite at the level of assault rifles or suicide vests. At least, not yet.

It's hard to know how or when to talk about disasters, because there are so many ways to get it wrong. Years ago, back when I was in college, I watched the Challenger space shuttle explode. A bunch of us had huddled around a TV on campus. Launches had become as routine as grocery shopping, but this time was a big deal because they had a teacher on board. Mission Control counted down, the engines fired, and smoke began to churn. A rocket the size of a twenty-story building lifted from the ground, leaving the embrace of scaffolding. As it arced toward the clouds, the great cylinder rotated in a lazy pirouette. If you'd wanted to draw a picture of hope and ambition, this was it!

Then came that stunning burst of yellow. The bundle split, and plumes of exhaust forked. The booster swerved like a bottle rocket, and debris rained into the ocean. There were no parachutes. The room went so quiet we could hear each other breathing.

That's when one of our profs piped up from the back. It was old Arnie, a bit of a gadfly. "Oh well," he cracked. "Shows what happens when teachers get mixed up in things."

Too soon? Just a bit.

And yet, how much time has to pass? When I was thirteen I wrapped a piece of string around the tummy of a rubber tarantula and tied the other end to the ceiling light in the bathroom. Then I balanced the creature on top of a cupboard door by the sink. It took some finessing, but soon that spider would swoop down over anyone messing with the knob. When my little brother toddled in there that morning, rubbing the sleep from his eyes, the shriek he produced could have shattered glass. Even better, because he was always groggy in the morning, I managed to reproduce the performance several days in a row. To this day, despite all my attempts to convince him how hilarious it was, all I get is a

glower. I understand: it's still too soon. I need to wait a few more years before he fully appreciates it.

Time is the best anesthetic. That's why people here can make jokes about the French Revolution or Napoleon. World War I is mostly fair game too, but WWII is iffy. The Algerian War? Uh, no, maybe don't go there. Humor at the wrong moment is like a root canal without Novocain. Maybe that's why in Paris the terrorists started by going after the cartoonists—the ones doing spoofs of the prophet Muhammad, joking about stuff from fourteen-hundred years ago. The problem? Simple. It was still too soon.

In recent years we've had a series of "events." At such times, the city hunkers down, flinching every time a car backfires. When entering my local shopping center I have to open my bags for inspection, and I unbutton my coat to show I'm not carrying. The Metro grinds to a stop whenever an umbrella is left unattended, and military threesomes stroll through the parks, armed with machine guns. It's all part of

Vigipirate—the security alert system that we try to take seriously despite their naming it like a cartoon buccaneer.

Luckily, my neighborhood is a low priority for terrorists. We don't have many museums or government buildings—places that might as well have targets painted on them. And while there's not much of a police presence, we have a natural defense system: parking is nearly impossible. Terrorists would have to cruise through the streets for hours before they unloaded. Most of the meters don't even work. And if they ended up dueling for a parking spot with a mother whose Renault was loaded with kids and groceries, well, let's just say I think we all know how that would end.

I'd like to believe I still have a heart rattling around somewhere in my chest, but it's weird how distance affects it. I'm able to watch horrors on the evening news—bad stuff going down in Africa or the Middle East—but after shaking my head in sorrow, I wander to the kitchen to whip up some pasta.

It's eerier when shit goes down close to home. One night on TV I watched a terrorist shootout unfold in another part of Paris. A bunch of masked men had stormed a concert hall, while some of their pals picked off patrons at terrace cafés. Television usually transports me to distant lands and times, but tonight the show was here and now, only a couple miles away. I opened my window and leaned over the railing, listening for gunfire. But no, all I could hear was traffic. On the sidewalk below me an old man walked a fat dog. A bus roared by. When I closed the window, I didn't even pull the curtains. Why bother? There was no danger here.

Then the text messages started to fly. Everyone in my circle was checking to make sure no one had taken a bullet.

But it turned out that one of them had. And that's when it started to feel personal.

I was on my own for a stretch, so at least I didn't have to worry about the safety of my family. But through somebody's mistake in judgment I'd been put in charge of a group of students. They were all Americans, coming to study in Paris while the country was in a state of emergency. For a few months, I was expected to play the grownup, helping them fix their verb conjugations and go to the theater. It was OK at first, but current events kept creeping in. There were more terrorist attacks—this time in Brussels. A manhunt in Paris ended in gunfire. Not long after, a guy with a knife carved up a police captain in the name of—well, it wasn't very clear in the name of what—and then he did the same to the guy's wife. The students looked to me for answers, but who was I to weigh in? When they asked what the hell was going on, I'd say, "That's a good question. Why don't we see what Molière had to say about it?" It was so much easier to turn to books, to hole up in the there and then. Here and now I'd probably make things worse. It would be the space shuttle all over again—a teacher messing things up.

Profs everywhere were having trouble. Sabine, who taught on the outskirts of Paris, had a breakdown. What was the matter? Some of her students supported the terrorists.

The crazy thing was, the same kind of stuff was happening in the US—nightclub shootings, machete hackings, you name it. The difference was, in Paris people got depressed, while in the US they got angry. Americans were buying guns in record numbers. Sales went through the roof. In the States people don't like to sit on their hands. They'd rather sit on a crate of ammunition. It makes you feel like you're doing something.

That kind of thing would never happen in Paris. Or so I thought.

One day in I ran into Cyril, the president of our building association. He was coming down the stairs, led by two cops. Cyril works as a theater director, and although he does some rather avant-garde productions, I've never felt they rise to the level of a criminal act. But maybe the *Comédie-Française* had its own police force, and if so, he might get twenty or thirty years for daring to do something interesting.

He wasn't wearing handcuffs, but Cyril is so skinny I assumed they'd just slipped off. But no, it turned out he was a free man. When he stopped to chat, the officers continued their descent.

"They knocked at my door," he told me, his eyebrows rising to where his hairline used to be.

"What for?"

"You have a minute?"

He invited himself into the living room and waved me over to the window, pointing at the building across the street. A couple floors up, there was a sliding door going out to a balcony. Strips of masking tape speckled the glass, each one next to a dark pimple.

"Bullet holes," he said. "The police say they came from this direction."

I pictured Cyril in his apartment, a sniper rifle at his shoulder, his eye pressed to the scope, lining up the sights.

No, no, it wasn't him, he protested, half-offended, half-flattered. He'd been cleared. The angle wasn't right.

"But then, who...?" My mind reeled. An idea loomed: *La dame du cinquième!*—the crazy hoarder whose dog left gifts for us on the landings. Maybe she had finally cracked.

Still, what could we do about it? If our neighbor had taken to eliminating us one by one, it would just go on the agenda for next year's general assembly of the building association. After all, rules were rules. And by next year, she might be a majority all by herself.

We never got to the bottom of that particular episode. The glass across the street was replaced one day, and it felt like we'd gone back to normal.

On the news they kept talking about French kids leaving the *banlieues* to go and join ISIS, where I guess they trained to return to Paris and creep up on customers sipping hot chocolate in cafés. At the same time, I was doing my own training, helping my students read French poetry and learn new words. I spent a lot of time hammering on language, trying to flatten the bumps out of my students' grammar. It made me feel safe—like there was one thing I might still be able to control.

But I was wrong. I couldn't control it. Not much. I had this one student, Maxine, whose French was pretty good because she'd learned it early. Great accent. Fluid. Huge vocabulary. But there were still screwball errors that popped and crackled. For instance, she had a problem with helping verbs. In French sometimes you're supposed to use *to have*, but at other times you trot out *to be*. For instance, if you say that you've eaten something, it's *j'ai mangé*. But if you've just arrived or departed, *avoir* becomes *être*, and you say *je suis arrivé* or *je suis parti*. Maxine kept saying *j'ai parti*, as if the verb *être* didn't even exist for her. I offered corrections, but it was like working with Silly Putty. I'd stretch her language the way I wanted it to go, but a few minutes later it snapped back to its original state. Weeks went by, and soon students who'd been much weaker at the start were passing Maxine by. She was stuck.

"Why can't I learn this!" she wailed.

I didn't know. She was a smart kid, and she handled all sorts of other things without trouble. In fact, learning didn't present a problem for Maxine. It was *unlearning* that was so hard. Years ago she must have been sick the day they covered *être,* and after that her teacher had never called her on it. Maybe he'd been grateful to get any past tense at all out of the students. Maybe he was lazy. Maybe Maxine was the star of his class, and he was so busy whipping the others forward that he didn't have time for spit and polish. Whatever the reason, she'd been saying it wrong for so long that nothing else felt right.

Like so much of education, language learning is a question of habits. You repeat expressions again and again until they're as comfortable as an old pair of shoes. And you'd better get it right the first time, because once those shoes are broken in, new ones will never feel anywhere near as good.

I told Maxine it wasn't her fault. Something had gone haywire in her French class years ago. It was another case of teachers screwing things up. I made a joke about it, but Maxine's eyes were welling with tears. I guess it was too soon.

All the same, she wasn't the only one repeating things that were wrong. Plenty of folks had similar problems. During all the terrorist attacks, the National Front kept yammering on about Muslims and Arabs as if they were the same thing, nudging both groups into the hazy category of terrorists. The more they repeated it, the more it sounded right, like some crazy verb conjugation. People were trying these ideas on for size and walking around in them. After a while they fit pretty well, providing support in all the right places. What a great pair of shoes, they thought.

Moreover, some of the politicians were really good at scaring you. Even people who lived in towns that didn't have any immigrants were jumpy. It was as if the National Front had balanced a fake tarantula on the door of the bathroom cupboard of the nation, and no matter how many times people opened it, they still shrieked.

Worse yet, my students wanted guidance. At first I thought they were looking at some capable person standing behind me, but when I turned to check, no one else was there. Because of my age or my job or my red pen, I'd been armed with something far more dangerous than a Smith & Wesson: credibility.

The problem was, students assumed I knew what I was talking about. If I went into class one day and said things like *j'ai parti* or *je suis mangé*, everyone would follow suit. Right out of the starting gate, they were inclined to believe whatever I told them, simply because someone had pinned a teacher badge on my shirt. I briefly considered putting this to the test. I was going to make up some French expressions—fun little idioms like *rich enough to fatten a bird's butt*, or *as mad as a Tuesday toad*. All I had to do was write these on the board, lead the class in choral repetition of their translation, and *voilà*, they'd be screwed up for life.

Because, after all, wasn't that what my counterparts were doing, with something even more dangerous than grammar? And I don't just mean the National Front. I mean the guys on the other side, too—the handful of radicalized imams who were promoting Sharia law and enforced veiling,

Too Soon, Too Close

225

Invisible

IT WAS AN EVENING DURING THE HOLIDAYS, and our bus halted to allow an old man in a threadbare coat to climb on board. He tottered down the aisle, his cane knocking against seatbacks, and as the engine roared, our grizzled newcomer tipped back, his free hand swirling madly before landing on the jacketed bosom of the young woman seated before me.

She gasped.

Back in the Midwest, a gentleman would sooner tumble into an industrial meat grinder than commit an indiscretion of this sort. And if you happen not to be a gentleman, or there's no meat grinder handy, bystanders will step into the breach, combusting you under their righteous glares, like an ant cooked under a magnifying glass.

In France, where they mothballed the guillotine in 1981, public executions are less common, and this leaves time for drama to unfold. The shabby man had now regained his footing, and the young woman's jaw had closed. What, I wondered, would happen next?

The answer: a Christmas miracle.

"*Je peux vous aider?*" the woman asked. *Can I help you?* She took him by the sleeve, guiding him forward till his hand latched onto the metal bar.

It was an astonishing act of clemency.

The man with the cane now sought a corner to stand in, choosing one already occupied by a thicket of shopping bags. His repeated attempts to angle his way forward recalled the efforts of a Roomba seeking a path through a forest of chair legs.

It was at this point I realized the poor fellow was blind, left to grope through the City of Light in a blackness worthy of the catacombs, as if the light bulbs of Paris had all burned out (requiring replacements of the screw-ass or Frankenstein-ass variety).

Many years ago I'd made a Boy Scout pledge to do a good turn daily, and because this promise bore a growing resemblance to the national debt, I seized the opportunity. Leaping forward to take his elbow, I guided my fellow man to the spot I'd just vacated.

He patted my arm in thanks. "Here I'll be out of the way," he explained in French. "Here I won't bother anyone." He had the accent of an old immigrant, maybe from Eastern Europe. Then his faded orbs latched onto mine. "The important thing," he announced, "is to be *invisible.*"

Now, I'm not the type to forecast the weather with tea leaves or converse with grandma through a Ouija board, but when a blind man stares into your eyes and claims he wants to disappear from a world he can't see, the message unfurls inside your skull like the contents of a fortune cookie. In antiquity, weren't all those soothsayers blind? And didn't they, too, speak in riddles?

What would it mean, I wondered, to go *invisible*, especially here? After all, more than anything, Paris promises eye candy—the seeing of sights, a feast of visions, vistas and views. The city is always lifting a hem, showing a bit of leg.

But imagine you can't see. People would gawk as you fumble with your cane. You grope for railings, and they snigger. Although the light is green, you wait patiently at the crosswalk, and they shake their head in pity. Incapable of *watching* the spectacle of Paris, you would *become* it. This explained the sags of the blind man's flesh. It came from the exhaustion of serving as a live exhibit. Time hadn't eroded his tattered clothes—*eyes had.* The unrelenting gaze of passersby had worn him down. His sightlessness could never escape notice.

My fellow traveler leaned in. A bit too close, frankly, but how was he to tell?

"Excuse me," he said. "Are we at Alésia yet?"

I craned to peer through the evening. The stop, named for the battle where Julius Caesar conquered the Gauls, was still far away. "I'll let you know," I promised, nodding to reassure him—only to realize that my nod would, in a manner of speaking, fall on deaf ears.

The bus growled forward, and I set to imagining a life of sightlessness in Paris, navigating the city's potholed pavement and garbage cans with a stick. Maybe the vibrations of the Metro would serve as a compass. There would be that jungle of aromas to orient you—diesel fumes and fresh bread and fish stands, not to mention, at this particular season, chestnuts blackening on makeshift grills. Like a bat, you'd triangulate your position by sound, listening for church bells and honks, the squeaking wheel of the mailman's cart, the piano scales plinking from that third-story window every afternoon at 4:00.

The bus slowed, and the man jostled against me once more.

"Alésia?"

"No, no. Just a bit farther."

A timid smile on his lips, he sank back to the corner, shrinking into his coat, doing his best to shrivel.

I could see it all. He'd always been the odd man out, the square peg, the misfit. Moreover, I *understood* him. How could I not? After all, I too had spent years making a spectacle of myself here. Anne and I had bought the apartment and turned it into a home. Like Oliver Twist getting delivered to the workhouse, we'd left our daughter on the doorstep of their educational system. When that wasn't French enough, I signed up for the building association, I mourned my neighbors at the same time I plotted my expansion, I embraced the bureaucracy of *notaires*, bankers, and brigadiers, I marched with protesters, I even dodged the terrorists!

And yet, despite everything, the guy who greeted me in the mirror every morning remained stubbornly American. Disappearing would have been such a useful skill.

Onward the bus rumbled. Outside, the white tower of the Alésia church flashed between two rooftops. The nondescript square lies at the edge of a southern neighborhood considered *populaire*—that is, one that has nothing to do with popularity, but everything to do with the populace and the working class. It's close to the highway that runs where walls used to be, fortifications keeping the riffraff out of the city—people like me and my blind companion.

Finally we shuddered to a stop.

"We're here," I sang out. "Give me your arm." I could picture it now—off we'd go, two blind men staggering down the street, helping each other out of sight. I'd already stepped down, beckoning to him, my twin, my brother.

"No, no," he said, flapping his hand. "Not my stop."

Not his stop? But then, why the persistent interrogation? Like the prophets of old, had he simply foreseen *my* future, where I would exit? Before I could ask, the doors closed between us, and the engine roared. My old Tiresias was replaced by a plume of exhaust.

For a moment I closed my eyes. Deep underfoot the Metro groaned. Above me church bells clanged. A siren bleated in the distance. And through the air came the aroma of scorched chestnuts. The world smelled of Christmas.

Sucking in the winter air, I patted my sides and straightened my gloves. Onward! Rich with the gift of this encounter, I could now...now...

I paused, patted my coat again, then my pockets.

Where on earth had my wallet gone?

I looked about for the bus. But it had disappeared.

Acknowledgments

"Of all the books about Paris," my agent said, her right eyebrow arched, "this is certainly one of them." Given such praise, how could I abandon the project? (Victoria, thank you; turns out you were right.) And now that I've nailed down the essence of the City of Light once and for all, haggard publishers can finally move on to other topics. I dog-paddle in the sea of their gratitude.

The award for forbearance goes to my wife, who had to experience most events in this book twice—first the living, then the telling. The award for moral support goes to our kids. Let's see how they handle sharing it. Carleton College somehow counted this venture as—wait for it—"scholarship." (I know, right?) Thanks to an administrative error, the Minnesota State Arts Board issued me a grant, and even though it was for a different book, I was secretly working on this one at the same time. Feels good to get that off my chest.

My editors at Travelers' Tales/Solas House, James O'Reilly and Larry Habegger, get the X-Ray Vision Prize for seeing what this book could become. To artist Liam Golden what can I say other than, "Hey, stop being so good! You're distracting from the stories!"

Finally, I burned through a pack of friends while begging for input, and I'm hoping if I plug them here I can shame them into answering my calls again. Top among them are: Eric Vrooman, Martine Reid, Greg Johnson, Becky Boling, Michael Kidd, Laura Goering, Doug Green, Bob Tisdale, Joe Green, Trudi Anderson, Kelly and John Wheaton, Carole and Ned Hancock, Mary and Bill Upjohn.

Did I forget you? Sorry. Please add your name here: _____.

About the Author

Scott Dominic Carpenter teaches French literature and creative writing at Carleton College (MN). Winner of a Mark Twain House Royal Nonesuch Prize (2018) and recipient of a Minnesota State Arts Board grant, he's the author of *Theory of Remainders: A Novel* (named to Kirkus Reviews's "Best Books of 2013," and a Midwest Connections "Pick") and of *This Jealous Earth: Stories*. His shorter work has appeared in a wide variety of venues, including *The Rumpus, Silk Road, South Dakota Review, Catapult, Ducts, Lowestoft Chronicle*, and various anthologies. His website is located at www.sdcarpenter.com.

Travel Literature

The Best Travel Writing, Soul of a Great Traveler, Deer Hunting in Paris,
Fire Never Dies, Ghost Dance in Berlin, Guidebook Experiment, Kin to
the Wind, Kite Strings of the Southern Cross, Last Trout in Venice, Marco
Polo Didn't Go There, Rivers Ran East, Royal Road to Romance, A Sense of
Place, Shopping for Buddhas, Soul of Place, Storm, Sword of Heaven, Take
Me With You, Unbeaten Tracks in Japan, Way of Wanderlust, Wings, Coast
to Coast, Mother Tongue, Baboons for Lunch, Strange Tales of World Travel,
The Girl Who Said No

Women's Travel

100 Places Every Woman Should Go, 100 Places in Italy Every Woman Should
Go, 100 Places in France Every Woman Should Go, 100 Places in Greece
Every Woman Should Go, 100 Places in the USA Every Woman Should Go,
100 Places in Cuba Every Woman Should Go, 50 Places in Rome, Florence,
& Venice Every Woman Should Go, Best Women's Travel Writing, Gutsy
Women, Mother's World, Safety and Security for Women Who Travel, Wild
with Child, Woman's Asia, Woman's Europe, Woman's Path, Woman's World,
Woman's World Again, Women in the Wild

Body & Soul

Food, How to Eat Around the World, A Mile in Her Boots,
Pilgrimage, Road Within

Country and Regional Guides

30 Days in Italy, 30 Days in the South Pacific, America, Antarctica, Austra-
lia, Brazil, Central America, China, Cuba, France, Greece, India, Ireland,
Italy, Japan, Mexico, Nepal, Spain, Thailand, Tibet, Turkey; Alaska, American Southwest, Grand Canyon, Hawai'i, Hong Kong, Middle East, Paris,
Prague, Provence, San Francisco, South Pacific, Tuscany

Special Interest

Danger!, Gift of Birds, Gift of Rivers, Gift of Travel, How to Shit Around
the World, Hyenas Laughed at Me, Leave the Lipstick, Take the Iguana,
More Sand in My Bra, Mousejunkies!, Not So Funny When It Happened,
Sand in My Bra, Testosterone Planet, There's No Toilet Paper on the Road
Less Traveled, Thong Also Rises, What Color Is Your Jockstrap?, Wake Up
and Smell the Shit, The World Is a Kitchen, Writing Away, China Option,
La Dolce Vita University

Other Books by Scott Dominic Carpenter

Theory of Remainders: A Novel. At fifty-two, psychiatrist Philip Adler is divorced, alone, and gutted of passion. When a funeral draws him back to his ex-wife's homeland of France, the trip reunites him with a trauma he has struggled to forget: the brutal death of his teenage daughter fifteen years earlier. Prodded by his former brother-in-law and stirred by the unspent embers of his marriage, he embarks on a mission to resolve lingering questions about this past, hoping to heal himself along the way. The search leads to a disturbed man who may hold more answers than anyone expects—if only Philip can hear what he's trying to say.

A suspenseful literary novel set in the lush backgrounds of Normandy, *Theory of Remainders* explores the secret ties between love, trauma, and language. Named one of the Best Books of 2013 by Kirkus Reviews. ISBN: 978-0988904910

This Jealous Earth: Stories. A man puts his beloved pets to the knife; a family prepares for the Rapture; a woman in a department store slips a necklace into her purse. Whatever the situation, the characters in *This Jealous Earth* find themselves faced with moments of decision that will forever alter the course of their lives. Always moving and often touched with humor, Carpenter's stories examine the tension between the everyday and the transcendent—our struggle to grasp what lies beyond our reach. Whether hawking body parts in a Midwestern city, orbiting through the galleries of a Paris museum or plotting sibling tortures in an Arizona desert, his characters lead us through a series of dilemmas of universal appeal. "Stories...that imbue the ordinary with the extraordinary" —Siri Hustvedt. ISBN: 978-1480172777